ROSES
How to Select, Grow and Enjoy

W9-BMH-036

Richard Ray
Michael MacCaskey

Contributing Editor: Gary Cromwell
Technical Editor: Robert Cowden
Photography: Michael Landis

Produced by
Horticultural Publishing Co., Inc.:
Art Director: Richard Baker
Associate Editor: Lance Walheim
Research Editor: Dan Burnett; Copy Editor:
Bud Childress; Production Editor: Kathleen
Parker; Design: David Conover, Judith
Hemmerich, Betty Hunter; Typography:
Linda Encinas; Illustration: Roy Jones;
Additional Photography: William Aplin,
Robert Cowden, Paul Forsberg. Cover
Photo: Michael Landis

NOTICE: The information in this book is true and
complete to the best of our knowledge. All
recommendations are made without guarantees on the
part of the authors, Horticultural Publishing or Price
Stern Sloan. The authors, Horticultural Publishing and
Price Stern Sloan disclaim all liability in connection
with the use of this information.

ISBN: 0-89586-079-1
Library of Congress
Catalog Card Number: 80-82532
©1981, 1985 HPBooks, Inc. Printed in U.S.A.
Revised Edition
9 8 7 6 5
Published by HPBooks
A division of Price Stern Sloan, Inc.
360 N. La Cienega Blvd.
Los Angeles, CA 90048

Roses are for People

The sight and scent of roses have attracted people for centuries, making the rose the best-known and most-loved flower in the world. It has played a part in our histories and continues to inspire gardeners and non-gardeners alike. It is difficult for a book to capture the essence of the rose and explain its place in our hearts and minds. But a book can present simple and practical methods for growing and enjoying roses. Once you plant a rose, you'll discover the essence of its character yourself.

The purpose of this book is to put you on the path of rose discovery. It will help you find the roses you want, get them started and keep them growing. Forget what you may have heard about roses being difficult to grow. You'll find that roses are surprisingly self-sufficient plants. Roses will return more to you for your time and effort than any other flower.

For the most part, the following pages deal with the great roses of today—the hybrid teas, grandifloras, floribundas, miniatures and climbers. For each of these rose classes, there are descriptions and photographs of the best and newest varieties. Old roses and shrub roses, plants that many find attractive both for their antique charm and their robust vigor, are also included.

The approach of this book is practical, but this does not mean the great beauty of roses is taken for granted. What is the power of a plant that for centuries has inspired every kind of poet, lover and artist, or anyone who really looked?

Poets, lovers, artists and the rose—The physical nature of the rose is easy to see. Its fragrance has been analyzed and its colors named. But the most important nature of the rose can only be understood by your intuitive senses. A rose seen through unprejudiced eyes is simply beautiful.

The rose is a symbol of character and meaning. It always implies the superlative, a pure character or rich meaning. If beauty is beyond the power of language, then it is "like a rose."

Fossils indicate that roses have flourished for some 30 million years throughout most of the Northern Hemisphere. Roses are common in the wild and will

The rose 'Double Delight' is pictured at left.

survive a rough transplanting far more readily than almost any other wild plant.

To date, some 200 wild species of roses have been found, identified and classified by botanists. Their colors range from white through pink, red and yellow. All have single flowers, meaning one row of petals.

From earliest times the rose has been a symbol of love, invoking the sentiments of the heart.

Sappho, a Greek poetess who lived during the 6th century B.C., is generally credited with naming the rose the "Queen of Flowers." She loved roses and wrote of them often.

The rose native to areas around Greece is *Rosa gallica,* simply called *the Red Rose.* It flowers once each year and has a sweet fragrance.

Records are sketchy, but when the Greek botanist Theophrastus talked about roses (about 260 or 270 B.C.), the cabbage rose, *R. centifolia,* was already ancient. Its origins had been long forgotten. This rose has many petals—literally "100 petals"—so it's most likely a hybrid, the result of generations of gardeners choosing and replanting only the most beautiful rose.

The Romans imported the cabbage rose from Egypt and Greece so they could have blooms year-round. Eventually they learned how to force winter bloom using hot houses, and considerable amounts of farmland were converted to rose gardens, an impracticality noted with despair by the Roman poet Horace. Emperor Nero gave banquets where guests reclined on cushions filled with rose petals and walked on floors inches deep in rose blooms. Rosewater filled the fountains. Queen Cleopatra is said to have had rose petals "knee deep" throughout the room where she first entertained Mark Antony.

With the decline of the Roman Empire, the rose almost acquired a bad reputation, being so closely associated with the extravagance and indulgence of the Roman rich. It survived in the churchyards and monasteries and became a symbol of pure Christian love. Roses were also an important herb of apothecary gardens. Many preparations were made from petals and hips for treating a variety of ills.

Roses are for artists—At first, artists used the rose carefully in ways prescribed by the church. An example is Botticelli's "Coronation of the Virgin," painted in the late 1400's. In this painting the air is filled with roses falling from heaven, symbolic of God's love.

The Dutch artists of the 1500's painted more naturalistic renditions of flowers, roses in particular. Jan Breughel the Elder was commissioned by a wealthy patron to paint a flower arrangement. He was not the first to represent roses in a natural way, but is credited with inaugurating the style of naturalistic flower painting, a style that dominated succeeding generations.

Interest in horticulture and improved printing techniques a century later brought another change. Botanical illustration became an art form in its own right, and began to merge with the naturalism explored by the Dutch. One of the most notable painters of this group was Pierre-Joseph Redoute. His three-volume *Les Roses* published around 1820 was an artistic and botanical masterpiece.

Redoute's paintings—watercolors on vellum—are wonderful rose illustrations and the standard by which others are measured. He has been called the "Raphael of the Rose." It was 100 years later when artist Alfred Parsons, illustrator of *The Genus Rosa* by Ellen Ann Willmot, did work comparable to Redoute.

Roses have long been a favorite subject of amateur and expert painters alike. Ruskin, in his *Modern Painters,* speculates why: "Perhaps few people have ever asked themselves why they admire the rose so much more than all the other flowers. Consider first that red is, in a delicately graduated state, the loveliest of all pure colors; and secondly, that in the rose there is no shadow except which is composed of color. All its shadows are fuller in color than its lights, owing to the translucency and reflective power of its petals."

A rose lover's progress—Rose styles and fashions come and go much the same as styles of clothing or even ideas. Individually, our idea of beauty continues to evolve, affected by what is in vogue and our continual education and growth. What makes a rose beautiful? Answers vary.

Roy Hennessey was one of the most outstanding rose lovers of a past generation. His rose nursery in Scappoose, Oregon, was long known for its high quality and integrity. His simple catalogs are collector's items today. His book, *Hennessey on Roses,* contains this most marvelous description of a rose lover's (likely his own) changing definition of beauty: "Almost always the beginning gardener starts with something flamboyantly colorful, for he started to garden under an urge to beautify his surroundings. Masses of color where before was only drabness or plainness fulfills his just-discovered need for more beauty in his life.

"After he has saturated himself with color, with great splashes of all the innumerable flowers whose greatest appeal lies in massed color and not in line, he progresses naturally to more appreciation of beauty of line, beauty expressed in the clean sweep of a petal point or the graceful carriage of a blossom on its stem. Then he seeks new loves whose beauty is that of form as well as color.

Right: An environment for artists: The climbing rose covering the arbor is 'Royal Sunset'.

"So to the rose, but usually beginning just the same. Most often our progressing gardener starts his rose experience with the largest, gayest roses he can find, delighting at the same time in the grace of the buds but avoiding the more delicate colors and small slender buds.

"He begins to find he has favorites, unconsciously selected. He analyzes his reactions, and in finding out why he has favorites he finds that it is the most svelte, streamlined buds that have won his heart in competition with color."

And so, the progress of rose love never wears out, no matter when your affair begins. The rose will always entice, always show something new or respond in a new way. This is true for amateur and expert alike.

Roses have an inscrutable charm that can fascinate us all. There is no question roses have been important in many of our lives. Language cannot define the beauty of a rose. It comes close only when coupled with the word and idea of love. Hence the definition of rose beauty that works best: Any rose once loved is a beautiful rose.

HOW TO KNOW ROSES

If roses are new to you, the next 6 pages are important. You may read them all at once, or refer to them as you need. Either way, they contain the basic information you need to get started with roses.

Many words are used to describe roses and their characteristics. Botanical in origin or simply traditional, their definitions contain the distilled wisdom of generations of rosarians. Knowing the "Rose Words," pages 8 and 9, takes you a long way toward knowing roses. They will also guide you through this book, rose catalogs and nurseries.

The classes of roses, illustrated on pages 10 and 11, are not complicated. They simply group roses with similar characteristics and habits together. Once you understand how classes vary, you'll have a much clearer picture of how to use roses.

For the curious, there is the "Rose Family Tree" on pages 12 and 13. How did our modern roses evolve and why? Here's a simple and graphic introduction to a complex answer.

Wilma Owings' rose garden includes more than 100 hybrid teas, with many floribundas and grandifloras, and miniatures tucked in wherever they can fit. "I love all kinds of roses, but the little minis are my favorites. There's something about the way the tiny buds open that steals my heart away." Two of Wilma's favorite minis are 'Starina' and 'Mary Marshall'. In 1978, Wilma's garden won three trophies from the Portland Rose Society: the top award for visibility from the street, the Royal Rosarians Top Award, and the First Award for a rose garden.

Wilma Owings of Portland, Oregon, cut this bouquet on the 20th of June, about 10 days after the spring rose show. "But," says Wilma, "I can pick this many flowers virtually any day of the season. This garden has supplied all the flowers for many a wedding."

Conveying delicate sentiments with the symbolism of flowers is an ancient tradition. But the shy Victorians elevated the practice to a high point. These are just a sampling of typical rose meanings of that time.

Rose language

Red rose: *I love you*
Cabbage rose: *Ambassador of love*
Deep red rose: *Bashful shame*
Single rose: *Simplicity*
White rose: *I am worthy of you*
Yellow rose: *Declining love; jealousy*
White and red rose together: *Unity*
Red rosebud: *Pure and lovely*
White rosebud: *Girlhood*
Burgundy rose: *Unconscious beauty*

Rose Words

The Botanists' Rose

Genus name: *Rosa* **Common name:** Rose
Family: *Rosacea.* Includes 100 genera.
Order: *Rosales*
Number of species: about 2,000.
Number of varieties: about 20,000.
Where native: throughout Northern Hemisphere.
Plant habits: thorny shrubs, trailers and climbers.

Anchor root. Heavy roots that serve primarily to stabilize the plant.

Anther. The top part of the stamen from which the pollen is released.

Balling or balled. When petals cling together preventing the flower from opening naturally. Most common in cool, humid weather. Most often occurs in varieties of roses with 55 or more petals.

Bare root. A dormant rose plant without soil around its roots. The way most roses are sold.

Basal shoot. A basal shoot is the succulent new growth that originates at the bud union. Leaves and thorns will look the same as the rest of the rose. This vigorous new growth should be encouraged, but you should pinch the tip when the cane reaches 18 or so inches high. See Sucker.

Bicolor. A rose of two colors, usually one on the front or inside and one on the petal back. For example see 'Piccadilly', page 87.

Blend. Two or more colors on both sides of the petal surface.

Blind shoot. A growing shoot that is expected to produce a flower but does not.

Blossom splitting, splitting or **split center.** When the central portion of the flower is divided into two parts and separated by a deep cleft.

Blown bloom. A flower that is fully open revealing stamens.

Bud. Either (1) a developing flower, or (2) synonym for eye.

Bud union or **bud head.** The swollen stem section at or near soil level where the bud of the top variety was grafted to the rootstock.

Callus. The healing tissue that covers a wound.

Calyx. All of the sepals, considered collectively, as one unit.

Cane. One of the three or four main stems of a rose bush. They originate at or very near the bud union.

Canker. A localized disease, usually on a stem, that often results in an open wound.

Chlorosis. Yellowing of normally green leaves. Caused by a lack of nutrients, usually either nitrogen or iron. Iron chlorosis causes yellowing of leaves in between the veins.

Crown. The bud union where roots join with the canes at and just above the soil level. Also, the top portion of a tree rose.

Dead heading. Removal of spent blooms during growing season to encourage more flowers.

Dieback. When a cane or stem dies back to a bud or another stem because of a pruning wound.

Disbudding. Removing secondary buds on a main flowering stem to divert energy they would absorb from the main flower. To be effective, disbud while the secondary buds are quite small.

Eye. A bud on a stem from which new stem growth will begin.

Feeder root. Tiny roots that absorb water and nutrients.

Foliar feeding. Fertilizing by applying soluble, nonburning fertilizers directly to the leaves.

Fungicide. A chemical used to prevent or eliminate fungus diseases.

Heel in. Temporarily covering the roots of a bare-root rose with damp soil or sawdust until they can be planted.

Hip. The fruit of roses. It ripens to orange or red in the fall and is known for vitamin C content. Includes the seed-bearing ovaries.

Insecticide. Chemicals used to control insect pests.

Joint or **node.** The point of a stem where a leaf originates. Always includes an eye.

Lateral. A stem originating from a main cane.

Leaf. A rose leaf is composed of smaller units called leaflets, and is attached to the stem just below an eye.

Leaflet. One part of a leaf. Most roses have from five to seven, but some have as few as three, others as many as 19. They are always arranged in opposite pairs with one at the tip.

Miticide. A chemical used to control spider mites.

Mosaic virus. A virus disease of roses that causes yellow zigzag lines of mosaic patterns in the leaves. Transmitted during grafting. Not contagious or curable.

Neck. The part of the flower stem nearest the flower.

Ovary. The swollen base of the pistil. See Hip.

Ovules. The base part of the pistil that after fertilization and ripening is the seed.

Peduncle. Botanically correct term for a flower stalk that supports a single flower.

Pegging. Securing long canes to the ground by attaching their tips to a peg driven into the soil.

Petiole. Leaf stalk.

Pistil. The female seed-bearing part of the flower. Each consists of the stigma at the tip, the style or stalk and the ovule in the seed pod.

Recurrent. Continual bloom. Synonym for remontant.

Recurve. How an individual petal will lay back, curving its edges downward.

Reflexed. A petal bent outward or backward.

Remontant. Flowering more than once per season, or repeat flowering. Used in the same way as recurrent. See page 48.

Reverse. The back surface of a fully expanded petal.

Rootstock. The species or variety rose used as the root system for the flowering top variety.

Self-cleaning. Spent flowers naturally *shatter* cleanly and fall to the ground.

Sepal. One of the individual segments of the calyx that surrounds the petals.

Spider mites. Tiny parasitic spiders that live on the undersides of leaves.

Sport. A naturally occurring mutation.

Spreader-sticker. Soap-like materials used in conjunction with pesticides to improve effectiveness.

Stamen. The male pollen-producing part of the flower. Anthers are at its tip.

Standard. A bush rose grafted to an upright stock. The same as tree rose.

Stigma. The sticky tip of the pistil that receives pollen.

Stipule. Small, green growths of various shapes at the base of the petiole or leaf stalk where the leaf stalk joins the stem.

Stub. The end of a cane that remains after pruning. Occurs when the pruning cut was not close enough to a bud or eye, or when it was not close enough to the cane or lateral from which it was removed.

Sublateral. A stem that originates from a lateral.

Sucker. A shoot arising from below the bud union. Its leaves, thorns and perhaps stem color will be different. Remove as close to its point of origin as possible. See Basal shoot.

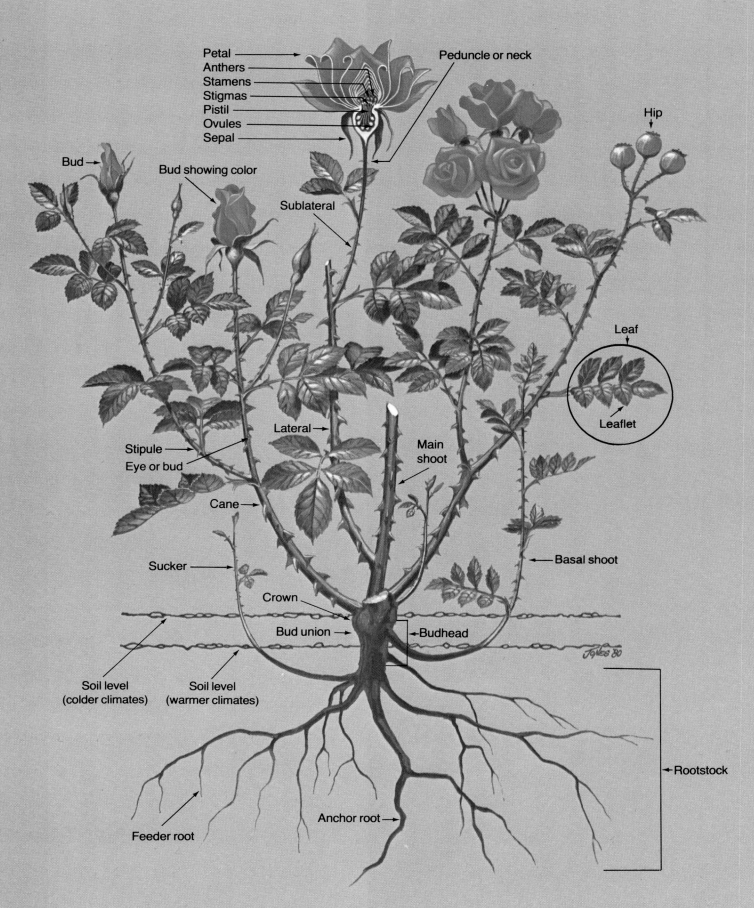

Petal
Anthers
Stamens
Stigmas
Pistil
Ovules
Sepal

Peduncle or neck

Hip

Bud

Bud showing color

Sublateral

Leaf

Leaflet

Lateral

Stipule
Eye or bud

Main shoot

Cane

Sucker

Basal shoot

Crown

Bud union

Budhead

Soil level (colder climates)

Soil level (warmer climates)

Rootstock

Feeder root

Anchor root

Jones 80

Roses by Class

Rose classes are convenient categories used primarily for cataloging purposes. But they are neither absolute nor unchanging. Class names imply basic characteristics of roses and, where similarities are apparent, tie the class to its parents. For example, floribundas are abundantly *floriferous,* meaning they flower freely in clusters. Hybrid teas are primarily hybrids of the tea rose, *Rosa odorata.*

The hybrid tea class, only 90 years old, was created mostly because rosarians could not agree whether 'La France' was a hybrid perpetual or a tea. The floribunda class was established just 46 years ago when it became apparent they were quite different from other rose classes. British rosarians still do not use the grandiflora class designation, because they do not believe there is enough difference between them and floribundas or hybrid teas to warrant the distinction.

The six most common rose classes, *miniature, floribunda, hybrid tea, grandiflora, shrub* and *climber,* are illustrated on these pages. *Tree roses* and *pillar roses* are not true classes. A tree rose, also known as a *standard,* can be made of virtually any kind of rose, and a pillar is a climber with a more restrained growth habit. They are included here to show the range of rose forms.

SELECTING A CLASS OF ROSE

First decide how you are going to use a rose. Its use will usually dictate a choice among roses of a specific class.

For instance, if you want a large background shrub, look to one of the shrub roses or, perhaps, to a grandiflora. A low-maintenance hedge of moderate height would most likely be found among the floribundas. A ground cover could be miniature roses planted in masses, or one of the wide-spreading rose species such as *Rosa wichuraiana.* A hybrid tea will produce the right kind of flower for a bud vase and may be used in many ways in the landscape.

Generalities such as these mark the usefulness of the class distinctions. A good way to find the rose you want is to begin here and choose a class, then select a color, pages 58 to 65. Details about the particular roses are given in the encyclopedia, pages 67 to 147.

Miniatures (Pages 137 to 147)
Miniature roses include all rose types, only in minute form, usually less than 12 inches tall. There are miniature climbers, trailers and perfect hybrid tea types. They are available in as wide a range of colors as their full-size brethren.

Use them for edging, low borders, ground covers and in containers.

Floribundas (Pages 97 to 115)
Hardy and disease resistant, these are the best all-purpose landscape roses. Most grow only 2 to 4 feet high, though a few will reach 6 feet. Climbing forms are available. Use them for borders, hedges, ground covers and in containers. Flower production is very heavy.

Hybrid teas (Pages 67 to 95)
These are the great all-around modern roses. Depending on the variety, their height can range between 2-1/2 and 7 feet, but most are 3 to 5 feet tall. Many are available in climbing forms, called *climbing sports.* Hybrid teas are the roses most often used to make tree or standard roses.

Grandifloras (Pages 117 to 123)
These large shrubs, growing to 8 to 10 feet tall, make fine background plants and produce many flowers per plant.

Flowers have characteristics of both hybrid teas and floribundas. They are only slightly smaller than hybrid teas, and occur in clusters like floribundas. They are vigorous and reliable flower producers. Many are fragrant.

PATENTED ROSES

A promising rose is grown for several years by its hybridizer before it is shown to anyone else. If he believes it to be superior, the rose is assigned a test number and distributed to gardens throughout the country. It is considered worthy of commercial release if it performs well for many growers in a wide variety of climates and conditions. As a new rose is being prepared for introduction, it is named and patented. The patent gives the hybridizer exclusive right of propagation for 17 years. But to rapidly increase the supply of a new rose, several growers will be licensed. They are required to pay a royalty to the patent holder for each rose sold. This cost is passed on to the consumer.

A patent in itself does not make a rose superior, but the best of all the new roses are patented. The patents on many excellent roses have expired so they are slightly less expensive. For instance, the patent on 'Peace' expired in 1963. Do not pay a premium price for a rose that is not patented.

Climbers (Pages 125 to 135)
Climbing roses do not "climb" naturally. They are simply very vigorous growers that produce long canes. Many are extra-vigorous mutations of hybrid teas, floribundas or grandifloras and are called *climbing sports*. 'Climbing Peace' is a climbing sport of the hybrid tea 'Peace'. The large-flowered climbers are more hardy. Unsupported, climbers will eventually form huge mounded shrubs.

Pillar roses (Pages 125 to 135)
In precise terms, a pillar rose is any rose trained to climb a pillar or post. Not a class of roses, it is a term that has evolved in general usage. Normally these are less vigorous climbing roses. Pillar training dramatically displays a climbing rose and also saves space, an advantage in smaller gardens.

Tree roses (Page 149)
Not a true class of roses, tree roses are important in the garden. All have three parts: rootstock, trunkstock and the flowering top part. Most commonly, hybrid teas and grandifloras are used for tops.

Tree roses are less hardy and need winter protection in all but the warmest southern and western areas.

Shrub roses (Pages 149 to 151)
Most of these are older varieties that lack color but are extremely tough. They are hardy and disease resistant. Height is usually 6 to 10 feet and shape varies. Some are fountain shaped; others more stiffly upright. New, more colorful varieties are introduced periodically.

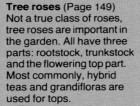

The Rose Family Tree

This is a very simplified approach to a rose family tree. The basic relationships were established by the Cambridge geneticist, Dr. C.C. Hurst, who was the first to study rose chromosomes. But few rose relationships are distinct—virtually every group represents thousands of crosses and backcrosses, both natural and man-made. The great changes began in the 1800's when the ancient roses of Europe were first crossed with the remontant Chinas. Our floribundas, grandifloras and hybrid teas are the result.

European Roses

Rosa gallica
French rose.
A variable and ancient rose, this is the prototype of all European roses. Both the centifolias and damasks are believed derived from it. It is very hardy, spreads by both seeds and runners. Flowers are rather large, flat and red with purple undertones; they appear once a year in June. Most are semidouble and *very* fragrant. A favorite of herbalists, the petals retain both color and perfume in *potpourri*.

Rosa moschota
Musk roses.
India or southern China are the supposed origins of this ancient rose. Early Europeans knew it well. It becomes an arching shrub with overhanging growth. Flowers are white, appear mostly in July, and are occasionally remontant. "Musk" odor is a honey-beeswax smell and most pronounced in the evening.

Rosa pendulina
Alpine brier.
A native of the Alps, the alpine rose is adapted to rocky, infertile soil. The stems are thornless. Crossing with the China roses in the early 1800's produced a group of hybrids known as the Boursaults.

China Roses

Rosa chinensis
Bengal, China rose, or Old Pink Monthly.
A wild, single once flowering rose where native in Asia. But through generations in Chinese gardens, a remontant, double-pink or double-red bush rose evolved. These roses are the source of the everblooming habit of modern roses. Ancient in China, the first were brought to Europe in the 1800's.

Rosa odorata
Tea rose.
An important group of tender hybrids with perhaps the most refined form and colors. The perfume of the flower is like fresh tea leaves upon crushing. Many are remontant. Tea roses were very popular until the more hardy hybrid teas were developed.

Rosa centifolia
The cabbage or Provence rose.
These are graceful, loose shrub roses cultivated since earliest times. Flowers are very double, usually a clear pink and are heavily perfumed. Dutch hybridizers of the 1700's introduced many hybrids.

Rosa damascena
Damask roses.
The name is derived from Damascus, the ancient Syrian city that is believed to be the origin of these roses. The perfume is very strong—the variety 'Kanzanlik' is the source of rose attar (page 52). The plants become 6 to 8 feet high; flowers are double, red, pink or white.

Portlands
Damask subclass. Recurrent bloomers. Gave rise in part to Hybrid Perpetuals. From Italy.

Noisettes
Also called *Champneys*. Hybrids of the China rose 'Old Blush' and musk roses. Climbers. Flowers pink to white in large clusters. Originated in South Carolina. Summer flowering.

Boursaults
Hybrids of China roses and alpine roses. Most are climbers.

Bourbons
Hybrids of China roses and Damask or French roses. 7 leaflets. Flowers red, medium size.

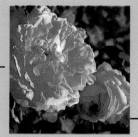

Rosa centifolia muscosa
'Comtesse de Murinais'

Hybrid Perpetual
'Baronne Prevost'
Also known as remontant roses. Mixed ancestry. Flowers white to pink to purple, large and double. Summer and fall bloomers.

Tea Roses hybrids
'Maman Cochet'—1893
Mostly from *R. odorata*. Suited to warm climates. Continuous bloomers. Large, high centered flowers with spicy odor.

Hybrid Chinas

Cultivated for thousands of years in China; first crossed with European roses in the early 1800's. Flowers appear two times or more in one season. Bright leaves, lightly scented. Flowers yellows to red. At right are a few notable examples.

'Old Blush'

'Slater's Crimson'

1500

1800

1850

Rosa foetida bicolor 'Austrian Copper'
Shrubs. Contribute to brilliance of modern yellow flowers in roses. Flowers mostly copper to yellow.

Rosa multiflora
Climbers to 10 feet. 5 to 11 leaflets. Flowers white, many in large clusters. From Japan and Korea. Crossing with the China roses produced the polyanthas.

Dwarf Polyantha
Hybrids of China and Polyantha roses. Small to large clusters, purple to red.

'La Marne' Polyantha

Floribunda

'Marina'
From crosses between hybrid teas and hybrid polyanthas, or hybrid teas and polyanthas.

Pernetianas
Brightly colored roses. 'Soleil d'Or', introduced in 1980, was the first. Yellow strains were included. Began introduction of yellow modern roses. Crosses between red hybrid perpetual and 'Persian yellow'.

Grandiflora

'White Lightnin'
Crosses between floribundas and hybrid teas. The first grandiflora was 'Queen Elizabeth'.

'La France'
First hybrid tea in 1867.

Hybrid Tea

'Bing Crosby'
Crosses primarily between older hybrid perpetuals, teas and China Roses.

'Hermosa'   **'Viridiflora'**

1900   1950   1980

Roses in the Landscape

Roses can be used in a landscape in a variety of ways. How they are used is largely determined by their class. Choosing what you want roses to do in your landscape will help you decide which class and variety to choose. The illustrations on pages 10 and 11 define the different rose classes.

The most common uses of roses are decorative. A hybrid tea or floribunda will bring color to a particular part of a garden. Or, carefully pruned standards will frame an entrance. These are just 2 of the many ways roses will work for you in the landscape.

Miniature roses can be used as a colorful ground cover or an edging. Anywhere you need a low border or a low color accent is a potential place for miniatures. If you have space, consider keeping miniatures in containers both indoors and out.

The size and hardiness of floribundas make them an all-purpose landscape plant. Use them along a wall, as a hedge or a border, or even as a ground cover. Their abundant color will enhance any garden.

Hybrid teas are used most often as individual accents or centers of attention. The size and shape of the blooms make them ideal for cutting.

The size of grandifloras makes them ideal choices wherever you need a large shrub, as long as the location is sunny. Grandifloras make fine background plants, and their flowers are excellent for cutting.

A number of older, tougher varieties of roses are classed as shrub roses. They can stand some neglect and are good choices for those corners of your garden that are difficult to maintain, but still need some color. There are varieties that form handsome, fountain-shaped mounds. Others grow upright to 10 feet.

New York—This garden demonstrates several good principles of landscape design. It includes a large, open space with an irregular border framed by a formal hedge. Only two rose varieties were used—the soft pink colors of 'The Fairy' are accented by the dark red 'Europeana'.

Tree roses, although not a separate class, can be used anywhere you want a small tree. They look especially well in a formal entrance or patio.

Pillar roses and climbers are trained to climb. They can decorate any sunny wall or post, but they must have support. Without it, they will sprawl haphazardly.

The basics of landscaping with roses are the same as with other plants. Before you put roses in your landscape, think of the overall effect. Using a lot of plants of one color will create a more unified, pleasing appearance than a collection of different colors. A good landscape is, above all else, connected with its surroundings. You know a successful landscape because it *works,* meaning it is tasteful, practical, interesting and attractive.

There are many ways to go about building a garden. The landscape professional is best equipped to plan and establish a garden over the short term. The "evolving" garden, one that develops over the years, is the special forte of the amateur and rose lover. The more loosely structured, informal garden is usually the best course for the home gardener.

Roses of one form or another are native throughout the Northern Hemisphere, preferring open and sunny locations. Therefore roses are suitable and appropriate plants for gardens throughout the United States.

If your garden has a rustic, perhaps rocky character, low and spreading roses such as *Rosa wichuraiana,* the miniature 'Red Cascade' or the 'Max Graf' rose will adapt nicely. On the other hand, a rural garden with a feeling of wildness that you would like to preserve will be complemented by the larger, more informal shrub roses. *R. rugosa* is native to coastal areas so is an excellent landscape shrub in those situations.

Regardless of site, building architecture may require a certain kind of landscape. Often, the more modern, geometric structures are best accented by more strident shrubs of stronger character. Of the roses, this would suggest the hybrid teas. If you are renovating the landscaping of a 100-year-old home, consider planting the roses popular a century ago.

Finally, balance all garden plans with simplicity. This does not mean the absence of interesting structures, plants or accessories, but the fitting and unobtrusive use of them. Simplicity is also achieved by planting masses of single varieties. A border planting of roses or other plants should never look like a catalog of everything available. Planted to a single, or a few carefully chosen colors, a border becomes a dramatic and strong statement. Ed Kaptur (page 28) echoes this idea when he says, "Use a lot of roses. Be generous."

Buy roses for a beautiful flower, but also consider roses for landscape situations. They will add interest to an otherwise ordinary landscape.

Oregon—Walter Regan takes advantage of two of the best uses of the rose. Top: Informal, colorful, low-maintenance floribundas line the front entrance. Above: Long-stemmed hybrid teas in the back are especially for cutting.

Rose Gardeners' Gardens

The next several pages are devoted to the words of rose gardeners and photographs of their gardens. The purpose is to show how people have used roses around their homes. All share an active love affair with the rose, represented by their beautiful gardens. They span a wide variety of interests, locations and styles. Experiences and opinions vary, but there are similarities. Their words and pictures prove there are many ways and many reasons to grow beautiful roses.

California—Floribunda roses are nearly ideal shrubs for municipal and commercial plantings. For all the color they add, a minimum of maintenance is required.

Michigan—The Kaufmanns have surrendered some lawn to roses. They grow miniatures and floribundas, partly for their hardiness, but mostly for their charm.

Oregon—A landscape needn't be complicated to be effective. This one employs mostly evergreens around a house painted in basic earth tones. The roses, varieties of floribundas, provide just the colorful accent necessary to complete the picture.

Two Years and 200 Roses Later...

Ken and Christine Pierson of El Cajon, California, may appear to be expert rose growers with years of experience. But actually, they got started just two years ago. Says Christine: "We went to a meeting of the San Diego Rose Society mostly out of curiosity. The people were so friendly and helpful that we stuck around. Because of them, I guess we started in a big way. We now have some 200 roses, only a few of which are duplicate varieties.

"We think the roses are great landscape plants and we like to exhibit flowers at local rose shows. You can see we don't have much else in our yard. There are 21 standard roses alongside the house with miniatures planted in front of them. We also use miniatures in front of most of our hybrid teas and grandifloras to cover lower canes. The miniatures we use most often are 'Magic Carrousel' and 'Sheri Anne'. We also like to use floribundas in our yard. 'Charisma' is fantastic. We also like the new 'Deep Purple' and 'Evening Star'.

"We really enjoy exhibiting the roses in shows. With the help of the rose society, we've been on the trophy table in every single show, from the novice category on up. Last March we won our first Queen of the Show Award with the new hybrid tea 'Honor'.

"It's funny because we were never much attracted to white roses, but we won Mini Queen of the Show with the white miniature 'Jet Trail'. Then at another show we won Best Floribunda with the white 'Evening Star'. Now we have won Queen with the white 'Honor'. You can be sure we love white roses now."

The Piersons used every bit of available space in renovating their landscape. Alongside the house are hybrid tea standards fronted by a border of miniature roses.

Roses fit into the Pierson landscape in many ways. Here, low-growing miniatures and floribundas planted in front of taller hybrid tea standards produce a wall of color.

Ken and Christine don't hesitate to pamper a rose. They know some of the older and more unusual roses may need a little extra care, but they find this makes the rewards greater.

Besides brightening the landscape, many of the Pierson roses are shown in exhibition. Since they began showing roses, they've had a rose on the trophy table of every show they've entered.

Growing Roses, from Coast to Coast

Jerry Scoville has been growing roses for some 20 years, first in Maryland and now in San Diego, California. The difference? Jerry says, "Well, for one thing, pest problems are completely different. In Maryland, you worry about blackspot and Japanese beetle. Here, it's mildew, thrips and mites. But it is interesting. I've grown many of the same roses in both gardens.

"I really don't have any favorites. There is a fragrant old *damascena* I enjoy very much. I also have a 'Climbing Dainty Bess' growing against a fence. It spreads out 15 feet in either direction and when it puts out its waves of bloom in spring, it's my favorite. It just covers the fence. Of the modern roses, I like 'Paradise' and 'Color Magic' very much. 'Climbing America' is another great climber.

"I grow several miniatures, usually as a border under and in front of the taller bushes. I've won awards with 'Starina' and I also like the new 'Holy Toledo'. 'Beauty Secret' and 'Party Girl' are other favorites.

"I've grown 'Tropicana' both in Maryland and here, and it's interesting to see the difference in flower color. I think it was a more vivid orange in Maryland.

"Several of the floribundas make excellent low-maintenance shrubs. I particularly like 'Europeana', 'Iceberg' and 'First Edition'.

"For fragrance I enjoy the light, spicy scent of 'Double Delight'. It is subtle and very pleasing to me. I also enjoy 'Mister Lincoln' and its stronger, Damask-type perfume."

Growing—"My growing methods are pretty simple. I've no secret methods or formulas. My roses are watered by both drip and spray systems. As you always hear, morning watering is best or else mildew may be a problem.

"Fertilizers, I figure, are all about the same. I usually buy according to price. If there is a sale on a premixed rose fertilizer, I'll use that. Otherwise I'll mix my own using urea and superphosphate.

"I have about 100 roses in the yard and one thing is for sure—there are always plenty for cut flowers."

In the landscape—The Scoville rose garden is a striking landscape feature when viewed from the patio as in the photograph below. "But," says Jerry, "Our love of roses came before any thoughts about landscape design. We wanted roses so we made room for roses. Still, there are few plants of as much utilitarian value. I've used floribundas alongside my house primarily because they are colorful, hardy landscape plants."

Jerry and Pat Scoville have adapted the uneven terrain of their backyard to roses in an admirable fashion. The mortarless rock wall makes an ideal raised bed when filled with improved soil. The layout is attractive and puts most roses within easy reach.

A Rose Judge's Rose Garden

Richard and Sue Streeper have been growing roses for almost 20 years. During that time, they have become very involved in local rose society activities. Richard Streeper is a past president of the San Diego Rose Society and both he and his wife have been chairmen of rose shows. Both are also members of the East County Rose Society and have been judges at rose shows. But their attitude is straightforward. Richard says, "Rose societies tend to be exhibition oriented, but we like all aspects. We do a lot of exhibition and judging, but we also like to visit pretty rose gardens and have a pretty yard ourselves. That's really more important.

"We probably have 200 varieties of roses and many favorites. Asking what are our favorites is a tough question; they change from year to year. Right now, 'Century Two', 'Pristine', 'Futura' and 'Honor' come to mind as outstanding roses in our garden. These are all hybrid teas, of course. We also have a wonderful landscape rose, 'Simplicity'. Let me tell you about it.

" 'Simplicity' is the low-growing rose planted all along the side of our house. It's from Jackson & Perkins and they don't even include it in their regular rose catalog. It is so easy to care for and does so well in mass plantings that they call it a 'shrub' so people won't expect it to be a typical rose. People have an idea of what a rose is and this rose is different. It was developed especially for landscape use and should be planted *en masse*. In fact, Jackson & Perkins sells them only in lots of a dozen or so, I think. We love it. It is absolutely trouble-free and always in color."

Growing—"We usually water with overhead sprinklers but use flood irrigation if the flowers are getting ready for a show. We think overhead is the way to go for an overall happy plant, because the leaves and roots get wet at the same time and the water cleans the plant. When the plants are clean, mildew and other pests can't become established as readily. We water in the morning. Overhead water in the evening will tend to encourage mildew even though that is not a problem if we spray. There is still a lot of disagreement about watering overhead, but in our experience it's by far the best.

"Our basic fertilizer is Milorganite. I'll use some ammonium sulfate along with it in the spring and usually add some superphosphate later in the season."

Above: Step through the old into the new. The old rambler commonly called 'Seven Sisters' covers the entryway to the Streeper garden of modern roses.

Right: Besides doing his own breeding, Richard Streeper is a member of a variety test panel for a major national rose grower. Here he inspects an unreleased variety.

Roses by Accident

Jack and Mary O'Neil of Upland, California, began growing roses ten years ago. Their first home had several kinds of plants in the yard, but of all of them, the roses grew the best. Jack explains, "We got into roses quite accidently. Before we came to this house, we had another house landscaped with a half dozen rose bushes, a half dozen camellias and a half dozen azaleas. I was new to gardening so I immediately ran out and bought books on how to grow each of them. We read each one carefully and followed directions, but everything just seemed to work best with the roses. As the roses thrived, so did our interest."

Today the O'Neils live with about 400 or 500 roses of some 200 different varieties. Jack says, "I have hybrid teas, grandifloras, floribundas, climbers, miniatures, old roses and moss roses. I enjoy growing all types.

"We always have loads of cut flowers. Anytime we go visiting we bring a bouquet of a dozen roses."

Jack is a Consulting Rosarian and active in both the local and national American Rose Society. "In fact, for the past three years, I've been the Pacific Southwest coordinator for "Proof of the Pudding."

Jack may seem an expert, but to him roses are just a hobby. Here's a little of what he has learned:

Favorites—"I could give you a list of five to 50. Of the hybrid teas, I do think 'Phoenix' is one of the best for this area. 'Honor', 'Century Two', 'Mister Lincoln' and 'Paloma' come to mind immediately.

"I can recommend two outstanding floribundas for the landscape: 'Orangeade' and 'Iceberg'. We have used both quite a lot in our front yard and they are just outstanding. The amount and consistency of bloom is incredible. 'Iceberg' is unique in that it needs no periodic grooming to look good because it sets no seeds or hips. 'Orangeade' does set seeds, but the two together make quite a show.

"From the miniatures I particularly look for good hybrid tea-type form and vigor. 'Mary Marshall' does very well for me. Others I like are 'Toy Clown', 'Starina' and 'Holy Toledo'.

"I have a lot of fun starting one or two hundred miniatures from cuttings each year. It's only so I can give one or two away whenever anybody comes to visit the garden.

"I buy roses everywhere by mail order from Armstrong, Weeks or Jackson & Perkins of course, but I also import quite a few roses from Canada. Also, there is quite a bit of trading of budwood between hobbyists. In other words, if I can find something I've been looking for, I'll bring it home and bud it up.

"I'm also involved in my own hybridizing program. Basically, I want interesting colors that will stand

The O'Neil rose garden is constantly changing. They grow nearly every type of rose—from old to new and from miniatures to climbers. They add as many as 30 new roses each year—replacing some, making room for others.

up to our hot summers. Lately I've been working toward some lavenders and mauves, and more recently, something in the yellow-orange blends that will take the heat."

Growing—"I water with one-quarter and one-half circle lawn-type sprinklers throughout the beds. Or sometimes I'll just put the oscillating sprinkler in there. I also fertilize the entire bed. I think that way the roses can develop a more extensive root system, big enough to stand up to the hot, drying winds that periodically occur here.

"I water in the morning so the bushes can dry relatively quickly. I spray pretty regularly, so it really doesn't make much difference when or how I water. Our climate is dry so we never have rust. Blackspot is nonexistent. Without spraying there will be mildew in both spring and fall, which I prevent with Triforine.

"Of course, we have the regular mites, thrips and budworms. Orthene solves most insect problems. I use Plictran for the mites.

"I don't believe in any one technique for pruning. I adjust my pruning to the bush. I just eyeball the plant and prune accordingly. Knowing the variety and how it grows helps. In general, I prune the yellows lightly, the others just pretty much as they need."

In the landscape—"My garden started out very organized. But every year I will buy 30 to 40 new varieties. There are always 10 or 15 old ones not doing as well as they should, so placing that many new ones is no problem. But the other new ones? They are grown in containers, or just squeezed in wherever they can fit."

Showing—"We exhibit roses an awful lot. We usually exhibit at four or five shows every spring and fall.

"Around mid-July I stop cutting off spent blooms, let them form hips, stop fertilizing and kind of force the bushes into semi-dormancy. This will build up food reserves in their stems. Toward the end of August I'll prune them moderately hard, feed and water generously. The roses think it's springtime and will grow with remarkable vigor."

Each year, Jack O'Neil starts as many as 200 cuttings of miniature roses, which he enjoys giving to visitors and friends.

Wherever the O'Neils go, they take cut flowers with them. One of their favorites to give friends is 'Double Delight'.

The grandiflora 'Olé' performs very well for Jack and Mary.

One Hour Per Rose Per Year

A former president of the Portland Rose Society, Reuben Newcomb of Portland, Oregon, runs his garden like a professional football team. "Any rookie that can beat out a veteran gets the job. I replace any plant when a better one comes along. Of the original planting, only 'Peace' has held its job. I judge them by their flowers, habit and vigor. For years I've been looking for a better white and a better yellow hybrid tea. With the introduction of 'Honor', I've quit looking for the better white. 'Honor' is it.

"The big bed in the back yard is mostly for exhibition roses. I have 24 kinds of hybrid teas in there. The best ones are 'Silver Lining', 'Peace', 'Fragrant Cloud' and 'Picadilly'.

"We grow a lot of miniatures in separate beds, and many hybrid teas. But actually, we like the floribundas best of all. We get more flowers and more enjoyment per unit of labor and space than we do from any of the other roses. They're good for massing, clipping, bringing in the house and for exhibition, too.

"Speaking of labor, people always ask me how I find time to take care of so many roses. The answer to that question is: I've kept careful records for the last three years. I have 350 roses and I spend 350 hours a year taking care of them. I spend just one hour per rose per year. Anyone can spend more time than that, but if they do, they're just puttering and enjoying themselves, not working."

Growing—"Portland has a moist climate and I've made it a policy to not grow any rose too susceptible to

Many of Reuben Newcomb's roses are hybrid teas and grown primarily for exhibition. Reuben is tough—he'll bump an old pro for a promising rookie. Of the original planting of 24 varieties, only 'Peace' has kept its place.

The vigorous shrub rose 'Dortmund' sprawls beautifully over Newcomb's front fence. The pinkish red rose in the background is the old polyantha 'La Marne'.

disease. Still, we will have occasional problems. 'Command Performance', 'Mister Lincoln' and 'Garden Party' are wonderful roses, but will mildew here. But controlling mildew is no big problem. I spray every 10 days or so with a combination of Phaltan and Benomyl. I'm experimenting with Triforine. Because of the mildew, we always flood irrigate.

"I fertilize with a tablespoon of 15-10-10 per bush the first of April, May and June. That's usually enough.

"Regarding pruning, I started out as a low pruner, but am now a high pruner. I'll trim the bushes in the fall to keep the wind from blowing them sideways, then wait until Washington's birthday in February to do any heavy pruning.

"When it's all said and done, there's one great joy about having so many roses. We always have plenty of cut flowers to give away. We furnish an awful lot of roses for weddings and neighbors. And there's still enough to bring inside our own house."

In the landscape—Reuben's landscape is continually developing. "I didn't start with a plan so the landscape has just evolved. Sure, it took a lot longer. But such a garden is much more satisfying to me; everything really fits together."

For exhibition, Reuben grows his roses in beds of 24 plants, with six of each variety. His search for a high quality white rose ended when 'Honor' was introduced.

Fragrance, Herbs and Potpourri

Margaret O'Neill of San Marino, California, grows roses for their fragrance. It was only three years ago that she planted her present garden.

"We had just remodeled and added the garden wall. I was replanting my herb garden and wanted a nice background for it. Roses were the perfect choice. The plants are attractive and I can use the flower petals in my *potpourri*. That's why they have to be fragrant.

"We got some background from a couple of books and the advice of other gardeners and chose eight roses: 'Sutter's Gold', 'Marmalade', 'Chrysler Imperial', 'Tropicana', 'King's Ransom', 'Mister Lincoln', 'Tiffany' and 'Fragrant Cloud'. These are all hybrid

teas and my most fragrant roses. I also planted some floribundas around my lamp post, and they have some fragrance, too. They are 'Sarabande', 'Sonoma', 'Cathedral' and 'Jazz Fest'. The Damask and other old, fragrant roses are wonderful, but grow too large for a small garden like mine."

Fragrant favorites—"Fragrance is, of course, my prime interest. Except for 'Chrysler Imperial', 'Fragrant Cloud' and 'Mister Lincoln', the perfumes don't last after drying. It does seem that the red roses are generally more fragrant. 'Fragrant Cloud' is such a sturdy and strong rose, and it lasts well after cutting. It would have to be my favorite. But I also love 'Chrysler Imperial' and 'Tropicana'.

"I pick the flowers when they are fully opened and place them in a vase inside for a couple of days. Their

petals are collected later and used in *potpourri*. I completely dry the petals on a drying rack made from screening. I've discovered that 'Tiffany' loses its color as it dries. It's a great rose but I plan to replace it for that reason.

"Naturally, I'm growing roses for a profusion of bloom. I want as many flowers as possible, not a few exceptionally good flowers. The way I grow them has just evolved. It's a matter of what's convenient and what seems to work. Because I use the petals, I will never use systemic insecticides. I use a spray intended for fruits and vegetables instead. I do water early in the morning to avoid mildew—usually with sprinklers but sometimes with a bubbler if the weather is extremely hot. I feed and spray about once every month."

For her *potpourri*, Margaret O'Neill cuts the blossoms when fully open and dries them on a screen.

Left: As a backdrop for the herb garden, Margaret includes eight varieties of fragrant hybrid teas. Clockwise, beginning in the upper left corner, are: 'Sutter's Gold', 'Marmalade', 'King's Ransom', 'Chrysler Imperial', 'Mister Lincoln', 'Tropicana', 'Tiffany' and 'Fragrant Cloud'. The last salmon-colored rose is the floribunda 'Cathedral'.

Roses in the landscape **27**

The Kaptur garden features a miniature rose border in the front with yellow pansies mixed in here and there, contained by a wall of grandifloras and hybrid teas. The close-cropped turf accents the color and just happens to be perfect for putting.

Most labor consumed by this garden is grooming—picking off the dead flowers, clipping or supporting a wayward branch.

An Old-Timer's Basics for Beginners

Ed Kaptur of Portland, Oregon, has been gardening since he was 14 years old. For 33 years, he cared for the nearly 10,000 roses in the Portland Rose Garden, one of the most outstanding public rose gardens in the world. And 10,000 roses is a lot of roses. Ed says, "I've probably pruned more roses than anyone in the United States."

Ed's advice to beginners is simple. "First, plant roses in a big hole, at least four times the size of their rootball. Use some soil amendment if your natural soil is too heavy or too sandy. Give the plants a chance! A good start will pay off ten times over. People squeeze the roots into a tiny hole and wonder why the plants don't grow. I say a good planting job and some occasional fertilizer and these plants will never stop. These new varieties are just incredible.

"My second piece of advice is to use a lot of roses. Be generous. If you've any room at all you should plant at least a dozen to a bed. I've got 26 'Sarabande' in one bed and 26 'Tropicana' in another. A great advantage of having a lot of one kind of rose is that there are always enough flowers for a bouquet. I've always liked bouquets of all one color. I can take a bouquet from the 'Tropicanas' virtually anytime of the summer.

"I use a mass of one color to accent a grouping of another color. You ought to see how a group of the white 'Honor' or white bicolored 'Love' roses look when they're bordered by the bright red miniature 'Tom Thumb'.

"I do believe that roses make the best possible border plants. Why plant annuals that always need replanting? A good landscape rose will bloom from early spring to late fall for years. I've got a 50-foot border in the back yard that has bloomed all summer long for the last 10 years.

"Last year I won Best Rose Garden from the American Rose Society. To qualify, you have to have at least 150 varieties of roses visible from the street. Of course, I'm a particular gardener. I keep my grass mowed short and all the edges are perfect. This lawn really makes a nice stage for the roses. It all looks like a lot of work, I know, but it really wasn't. This garden has evolved over the years and now that it's in shape, it doesn't take much time."

Ed's side yard includes a dramatic border of 'Sarabande' and a variety of miniature roses. The circular bed is the grandiflora 'Love'. The nearest rectangular bed is planted with the hybrid tea 'Tropicana'.

This meticulous garden evolved over the years and is surprisingly easy to maintain.

Flowing curves, clean lines and a bright green lawn add continuity and provide accent to the award-winning Kaptur garden.

Roses Like to Grow

No matter what you have heard, growing roses is not difficult. Rose gardening is too often considered reasonable only for the rare individuals with plenty of time, energy and know-how. "Roses need too much work" is commonly heard. Actually, the opposite is true. Meet their most basic needs—sun, water and occasional fertilizer—and you'll get a lot of flowers.

It is true that the more you indulge a rose, the more it will give. Leaves will be more attractive and healthy if you fertilize and spray for pests. The more leaves, the more flowers. But with absolutely minimal care, you will still have plenty of roses.

If you water and protect new plants for the first year, in all but the most inhospitable climates, you will have roses from then on. Roses are among the toughest of all plants, and most will grow and flower despite what is or *is not* done to them.

All plants have some enemies, and roses are no exception. But protecting roses from pests needn't be burdensome for they will survive without it. The effort should be made only if you want that extra quality.

If you don't spray for aphids when they appear on schedule in early spring, you'll have fewer spring roses. But by summer, the aphids will be gone and there will be flowers.

Blackspot disease is a problem only where the growing season is rainy and wet. If this is the case, you should spray every week to ten days. Even if you spray only once in early summer, your plants may not bloom in the fall, but there will still be spring flowers.

For roses, deep, generous watering is far more important than regular spraying. Leave the hose on low and let it soak. Or, leave the sprinkler on for however long it takes to wet the soil 1-1/2 feet deep.

If the prospect of growing roses worries you, think only of the basics. Plant where there is good exposure to sun. Don't skimp on the planting hole. Water generously, fertilize, prune and protect. These few steps will lead you to success.

Techniques of growing roses can assume an infinite number of variations. But all are based on these four simple steps.

Protect

Planting

Dig a planting hole about 2 feet wide and 1-1/2 feet deep and refill it with amended soil. Form a cone or mound of soil with your hands to hold the roots.

Examine the roots and trim away any that are damaged, shriveled or too long to fit into the hole without bending.

Position the rose over the soil cone and check height. Spread the roots over the cone and cover with soil. Make soil level slightly above bud union in climates of subzero winters. Where winter temperatures are above freezing, place the bud union 1 to 2 inches above soil level.

Growing beautiful roses depends on growing good roots. Your first opportunity to promote vigorous root growth is when you plant. A healthy well prepared planting hole is perhaps the single most important step toward ensuring a healthy rose.

When to plant—This should not be a problem because the time you are able to obtain a bare-root rose is the right time to plant. Local nurseries will announce their bare-root season and mail order nurseries will ship at the proper planting time for your area.

The best time to plant will vary somewhat by region. In the warm Southwest, roses will be available in the nurseries from December to February. Where soil freezes, roses should be available at the earliest spring planting time.

Bare-root roses—It is best to plant bare-root roses as soon as they are brought home. If this is not possible, keep the roots wrapped and moist and place your plant in a cool, dark location. Kept this way, bare-root roses can last about a week.

Before planting, soak the bare root for several hours in a bucket or tub of muddy water. This enables the bush to absorb as much moisture as possible. The mud will coat the roots and protect them from drying.

Where to plant—The *ideal* location for a rose garden is a spot with an eastern exposure that provides at least 6 hours of sun a day. The land should be sloped so that air and water drainage are excellent. Trees and shrubs that might compete for water and nutrients should be planted several feet away. Morning sun is preferred so that the rose leaves will be dried of dew as soon as possible. This provides an extra margin of protection from blackspot and mildew.

But do not let the absence of an ideal location discourage you. Even if the only place you have doesn't seem very promising, try anyway. Roses are much hardier than you might think. Any loss would be small compared to potential gain.

Soil—Roses grow well in all kinds of soil. However, both clay or sandy soils can be improved by adding some kind of organic matter—compost, peat moss, manure or wood by-products. These amendments in a clay soil will prevent compaction and enhance air circulation. A sandy soil with added organic matter retains more water and nutrients.

If you are going to plant many roses, a soil test can provide insurance against failures caused by poor soil. Most importantly, it will show the pH (acid-alkaline balance) of the soil. Roses do best with a pH of 6.0 to 7.0. If your soil is too acid or too alkaline, follow the

Once proper position is established, begin adding soil around roots.

Slowly add the soil and firm it around the roots. The bush should be firmly anchored when planting is completed.

Water thoroughly to settle the soil and to bring soil particles into close contact with the roots. After soaking the root area, build a soil mound over the bud union to protect it from a late cold snap. Mounding will also help preserve moisture in the canes. When new growth is 1 to 2 inches long, wash the mound away with a gentle stream from a hose.

instructions on page 35 to improve conditions. Soil tests will reveal the cause of sticky clay soil, a high sodium content, which is easily remedied by adding gypsum. A soil test will also show the relative nutrient balance of the soil.

If possible, amend soil in the fall to prepare for spring planting. By spring, a new soil equilibrium will be established. The planting job will be much easier and your new roses happier. If this is not possible, soil can also be improved in spring at planting time.

Spacing—Proper spacing will allow plenty of room for the roses to grow, for their roots to spread and for you to work around them. Typically, roses are planted 2-1/2 to 3-1/2 feet on center. In the South and West, where growing seasons are longer, you might add a little more room. Space plants a little closer where seasons are shorter. Rose bushes can always be reduced in size by pruning if they become crowded.

Dig a big hole—A proper size planting hole for a rose—bare root or container—is about 2 feet wide and 1-1/2 feet deep. This will permit wide-spreading root growth and good drainage.

CONTAINER ROSES

Roses in containers become available later in the spring and usually are in stock at nurseries through summer. They can be planted any time and do not need soaking before planting.

Follow the steps above when planting a container rose. Be sure to remove the root ball from the container very carefully so as not to damage existing feeder roots. A rose in a fiber container may be planted pot and all.

TRANSPLANTING

Roses that have been long established can be transplanted without too much difficulty. The time to transplant is when the plant is dormant or nearly so, in late winter or early spring. At this time there are few leaves for the roots to support, the climate is mild and the most vigorous growth period of the year is about to begin.

Prune the bush hard, leaving 3 to 6 canes of 3 to 4 buds each. Push your shovel into the soil at about 12 inches from the crown all around the bush. It may be necessary to dig away some soil so the shovel can reach deeper. Periodically push down on the shovel handle to lift the bush from the ground. After some working in this manner, the plant will come free. Carefully lift the plant from the base so the roots are not damaged unnecessarily. Replant as you would a new bush.

Watering

If your soil is heavy clay, water penetration is slow. A confining basin prevents runoff and allows the water to soak in.

A simple bubbler attachment threads to the hose end. Such devices allow a high volume of water to pass without splashing or eroding the soil.

Drip irrigation is the most water-efficient method. It also helps limit the spread of moisture-related diseases. If you use a drip system, allow 3 emitters per bush so that the entire root system is soaked.

Any method that lets you wet the soil to a depth of 1 to 1-1/2 feet is the best way to water. Use your choice of sprinkler, hose, bubbler or drip watering system.

The only way to be sure that the water is penetrating deeply is to check. Test your soil with a moisture tester with a long probe, a soil probe or a small shovel. The day after watering, the soil should still be moist to a depth of at least 1 foot.

Wetting sandy soil to the proper depth will require about 1 inch of water. Clay soil requires about 3 inches of water. Most soils will need an amount somewhere in between. If you water with a sprinkler, use a rain gauge to determine when an adequate amount of water has been applied.

Often we hear that you should avoid wetting leaves of roses during watering because they are susceptible to diseases encouraged by moisture. However, if you spray for disease, overhead watering can actually be beneficial. Water cleans the leaves of dust and air pollution and discourages spider mites. Some growers report that frequent washing of leaves with a mild soap or wetting agent solution reduces mildew problems. But if you choose not to spray, and leaf diseases are a serious problem, excessive leaf wetting is not advised.

How often to water—As a general rule, roses should be watered once a week throughout the growing season. But there are many variables that may extend or shorten the interval. During the very hottest part of summer when the roses are in flower, you may want to water every day. If weather is mild and the soil mulched, the soil may retain adequate moisture for two or three weeks.

Time of day—Morning is the best time to water roses. Leaves dry quickly, discouraging diseases. If you spray regularly for blackspot and mildew, water anytime.

Mulch—A mulch is a layer of insulation laid over the soil. It may be any one of many different materials—rock, plastic, wood chips, compost and bark for example. They all moderate soil and root temperature and significantly reduce water evaporation and weed invasion. Plastic is very inexpensive yet effective, rock is long lasting, and bark is most attractive. Any organic mulch will eventually decompose, adding humus to the soil.

FEEDING

Roses are strong plants. Given only cursory care, they will survive and produce flowers. Different roses may require different amounts of care, but most garden roses require regular feeding. There are many ways to go about it. Find the program that makes sense to you—one that is convenient, easy and works.

Feeding

Apply fertilizer according to label directions or the guidelines on page 36. Too much fertilizer can cause as many problems as too little. Always apply fertilizer to moist soil.

Cultivate so that fertilizer is well mixed with the soil. Left exposed on the surface, many fertilizers dissipate and effectiveness will be reduced.

Water thoroughly. This is important for two reasons: It helps break down the fertilizer and nutrients can be absorbed by the roots only when soil is moist.

What roses need—Nitrogen, phosphorus and potassium, or N-P-K, are the primary nutrients roses require for proper growth.

Nitrogen is a component of all proteins, so it's essential in relatively large quantities. If your rose receives too little, the leaves will yellow and growth will stop. If it receives too much, growth is overly succulent and the plant will be susceptible to disease. Water carries nitrogen away from the root zone and plants require large amounts to stay healthy. For these reasons nitrogen needs to be replenished continually.

Phosphorus is a critical element. It promotes sturdy stem and root growth, early maturity and good flower production. Plants deficient in phosphorus will be stunted and leaves sometimes have purplish edges. Phosphorus does not move in the soil, so it's best to incorporate it at planting time. You can add phosphorus to a mature plant with 1-inch deep holes in the ground just inside the plant's drip line.

Potassium, or potash, is the third important nutrient roses draw from the soil in relatively large quantities. Like phosphorus, it is crucial to enzyme processes. Deficient plants are weak, stunted and may have brown leaf margins.

Whether your soil is acid or alkaline depends primarily on where you live. In either case, it significantly affects your fertilization program. East of the Mississippi, soils are acid and need regular liming. Western soils are typically alkaline and can be acidified by many materials, primarily sulfur. The degree of acidity or alkalinity is reflected by the pH scale. A pH of 7.0 is neutral, below 7.0 is acid and above 7.0 is alkaline. Roses are not overly sensitive to pH, but grow best with a pH between 6.0 and 7.0. Soil pH significantly affects nutrient availability, particularly phosphorus, iron and other micronutrients. A slightly acid soil ensures optimum availability of important nutrients.

Soil testing—Local agricultural colleges or private laboratories can test your soil for nutrient content and pH. They will also recommend corrective measures on the basis of the test. Simple home soil testing kits can also be used for determining pH.

SELECTING FERTILIZERS

The essential nutrients are the same whatever their source. Roses do not prefer one source over another. They don't distinguish, for example, between nitrogen from blood meal or ammonium sulfate. However, different fertilizers may have side effects that affect soil chemistry an infinite number of ways. Many gardeners find that alternating different kinds of fertilizers works best.

Fertilizers are classified as either organic or inorganic. Organics include manures, compost and other plant or animal residues. Usually, their nutrient content is low, their relative cost high, and soil-improving aspects high. Most gradually acidify soil and add humus. In fact, humus is usually their most important contribution to the soil.

Inorganics are manufactured from basic elements. Most are simple salts that are immediately available to plants after slight modification by soil microbes. They are generally more concentrated and less expensive than organic fertilizers.

Inorganic fertilizers are available in a variety of forms. All are clearly labeled with three numbers, such as "10-10-10." These numbers are the percentages in the mix of the three primary nutrients plants need: nitrogen, phosphorus and potassium. A 10-10-10 fertilizer is 10 percent nitrogen, 10 percent phosphorus and 10 percent potassium. It contains 30 percent total nutrients and 70 percent filler. A 20-20-20 fertilizer is twice as concentrated and you would therefore use only half as much. This is one way to compare cost—how much nutrient for the money.

Granular fertilizers are the most common inorganic type. They are partially soluble and one application lasts 2 to 4 weeks. Most are not very concentrated, so the cost may be relatively high. Time-release fertilizers last the longest. One application may last an entire season. This adds to their convenience, but also to their cost. Soluble salt fertilizers such as RapidGro and Hyponex are completely soluble in water and immediately available to the plant. Cost is high, but many growers appreciate the fast action. Urea (46-0-0) and ammonium sulfate (21-0-0) are single element fertilizers. These are the most concentrated and most economical of all. However, they are often available only in larger quantities so are not practical if you have only one or two roses. Manures may also be used as fertilizers, but their prime benefit is as a soil conditioner.

Most rose growers use granular fertilizers, supplementing them with organic and soluble fertilizers. Whatever kind of fertilizer you choose, water deeply so that the fertilizer will enter the soil and reach the entire root system.

When to feed—One advantage of a fertilizer specifically intended for roses is that it includes directions right on the label. Generally, these directions call for feeding once a month throughout the growing season. The amount to apply will vary with the concentration as shown in the chart on this page. A soluble fertilizer with 10 percent nitrogen should be applied at rates between 1/4 and 1/2 pound per bush per month.

Fertilizer Sources

Fertilizer	Comments
Nitrogen (N)—Nitrogen is the most important nutrient and roses need a regular supply. Apply monthly, spring through summer. Apply to moist soil, cultivate, water again.	
10-10-10 (or similar) plus micronutrients, often called "Rose Food."	Effective, safe and convenient, but relatively expensive. Follow label directions.
21-0-0, ammonium sulfate	Acidifying action useful in western soils. Available in larger quantities. Fast-acting. Inexpensive. Use about 1-1/2 pounds per 100 square feet.
46-0-0, urea	Concentrated, soluble and inexpensive. Use about 1/2 pound per 100 square feet.
Dry chicken manure	Awkward to handle but very beneficial. Improves soil and supplies nutrients. Cost varies with availability. Use about 14 pounds per 100 square feet.
Dry steer manure	Many beneficial soil effects, but plenty is needed for use as a fertilizer—about 50 pounds per 100 square feet. Cost depends upon availability.
Phosphorus (P)—Incorporate at planting time or in holes around drip line. Adjust pH until slightly acid to improve availability.	
0-20-0, superphosphate	The best source of phosphorus for roses because it is somewhat more soluble. Inexpensive.
Bone meal	Low solubility and slow acting. Inexpensive.
Potassium (K)—Most potassium fertilizers are readily soluble. Use on a regular basis.	
0-0-50, potassium sulfate	The best source of potassium because it is less salty than other common forms. Inexpensive.
13-0-44, potassium nitrate	Supplies nitrogen as well as being a good source of potassium. Relatively expensive.
Sheep manure	Improves soil and has slight amounts of other essential nutrients, including 3 percent potassium. Cost varies.

Pruning

Pruning roses is a very simple matter and need not be the source of confusion or worry that it often is. First, obtain some sharp pruning shears. If your bushes are large, long-handled loppers and a small saw might also be helpful. Gloves are a necessity for many rose pruners, but others don't like the clumsy feel. Whatever your preferences, having the right tools will make the job easier, perhaps even enjoyable.

When to prune—The best time to prune is in spring just as the buds are beginning to swell. At this time, it is easy to distinguish between healthy and dead wood. You will also be able to see how the plant is intending to grow. Roses may also be pruned in fall. Excessively tall canes that might be damaged by whipping about in strong winter winds should be shortened. Also, a shorter bush is easier to wrap and protect from cold. The risk of fall pruning is that it may promote succulent new growth that will be very easily damaged during winter.

Roses that flower once a year should be pruned just after they bloom. This includes climbing roses, ramblers and most of the old garden roses.

How much to prune—Rosarians frequently differ about how "hard" or far back to prune. If winter damage has been extensive, you may have no choice but to prune to within a foot or so of the soil. In general, weak-growing varieties can be pruned more heavily than strong-growing varieties. Hard pruning is often practiced by growers looking for fewer, more perfect roses. Light pruning will allow a bush to grow to its natural size and shape. Lightly pruned roses will produce more flowers that are slightly smaller than heavily pruned plants.

The advice to prune hard, moderately hard, medium, or lightly may be outlined as follows:

Hard—Thin out all but 3 to 5 canes and prune these back to leave 2 to 3 eyes on each shoot.

Moderately hard—Thin out all but 3 to 5 canes and cut back to 5 or 10 eyes.

Medium—Thin out to 4 to 7 canes and cut back about one-half their length.

Lightly—Thin out to 4 to 7 canes and remove their tips.

As a general guide, remove about one-third to one-half of last year's growth. For most hybrid teas, this is the same as 5 to 10 eyes per cane. Remaining canes should be at least as thick as a pencil.

THE BASIC PRINCIPLES

There are many different kinds of roses and special pruning methods have evolved for each. Some rosarians have ignored the traditional recommendations and have created pruning methods for their own purposes. But the following principles will keep you on the right track whatever kind of rose you face.

• Remove dead canes to the crown. Dead canes will be brown and shriveled both inside and out. Removing them is the first operation when pruning any rose. Use a saw if necessary.

• Remove portions of canes damaged by frost. Winter damaged wood is sometimes hard to see. Wait until the buds begin to swell. When you cut through a cane, the wood should be white clear through. If there is any brown discoloration, remove more of the cane.

• Remove all of the weak, thin, spindly growth that tends to crowd the center of the bush. Or, as some rosarians say, "Open the center." Remove these stems and twigs all the way to their source, leaving no stubs.

• Remove any suckers. These are the extra-vigorous shoots rising from the rootstock below the bud union. Suckers are usually easy to spot—the growth has a different color and character with leaves that are distinctly different. Suckers should be removed completely, not just clipped off where they emerge from the soil. Dig or move soil away until you can see where the sucker is connected to the trunk. Hold it close to the trunk and pull downward to break it off. This will remove any adjacent buds as well. Young suckers will pull away easily. If you clip them off above the soil, they will continue to sprout and make another, more dominant rose bush right in the middle of the one you want. (See page 38 and 39.)

• Always cut at an angle about 1/4 inch above an outward facing bud. The angle should slope away from the bud. A cut made at this point will heal rapidly and water will drain away from the bud. No stub—a point of entry for disease—will develop if you cut close to a bud.

Usually you should cut to a bud that points up and away from the crown or center of the bush. Pruning directs growth and roses should be directed to form an open-centered, vase-shaped plant. However, some roses may tend to sprawl too widely. In such cases prune to an inward facing bud, directing growth in a more appropriate direction.

The beneficial effects of wound sealers are overrated for most trees and shrubs, but not for roses. Cut rose canes can lose substantial amounts of moisture quickly, especially when days turn hot. Freshly cut canes are also favorite entry sites for boring insects. Use a dab of white glue, shellac or similar nontoxic sealer to help prevent drying.

Pruning

1. Unpruned bush is twiggy, crowded in center with old, non-productive canes and dead canes that should be removed.

2. All final pruning cuts are made at an angle about 1/4-inch above an outward facing bud.

5. Vigorous canes are cut back approximately one-half their length.

6. Remaining canes are pruned to the same height.

3. Dead canes are removed to the base.

4. Weak and poorly positioned canes are removed.

7. Stubs too large for the loppers are cut flush with a small pruning saw. Seal large pruning wounds.

8. The pruned bush is open and has a balanced structure. Treat the ends of these large canes with a wound sealer.

Rose Pruner's Notebook

Hybrid teas—Prune to maintain 3 to 6 strong, healthy canes. Newer plants may not be able to maintain 6 canes. The canes should be uniformly spaced, ideally forming a vase shape. Old, non-producing, rough gray canes are removed at the bud union. Remove overlapping interior growth to allow light penetration and good air circulation.

Grandifloras—These are pruned just as hybrid teas, but most are more vigorous and may support as many as 8 structural canes. For cut flowers for the home, multiple bloom clusters might be preferable. For exhibition purposes, fewer, more vigorous canes might work better.

Floribundas—Most are low growing and tend to produce a twiggy interior growth that should be removed. Retain 6 to 8 canes and try to keep the plants open with plenty of room for new flower clusters to develop.

Large-flowered climbers—Shorten flowering laterals to 3 to 6 inches or 3 or 4 buds. Remove faded flowers of repeat-flowering kinds to hasten second bloom. Best flowering laterals come from 2 and 3-year-old canes.

Climbing sports—Long-lived canes produce lateral growths from which flowers arise. Shorten these laterals to 3 to 6 inches. Remove faded flowers to hasten repeat bloom.

Ramblers—Remove 2-year-old canes to their origin after flowering.

Miniatures—Prune essentially the same way as the larger roses. Hanging baskets are trimmed to the edge of the basket and the crown is flattened.

Tree roses—Always remove any growth from the trunk, below the upper bud union. Principles of pruning are the same, but the plant is at eye level and an attractive, balanced structure is more important. Check the support stake to make sure it is in good condition and not rubbing or chafing the plant.

Shrub roses—Prune only to shape when young. When mature, remove twiggy growth and very old canes. In general, most need little pruning. Prune old garden roses by removing the oldest canes and shortening the others by about one-third.

SUMMER PRUNING

Disbudding, cutting flowers, dead heading and grooming are the pruning chores of summer. Disbudding is the way to develop full sized flowers, one to a stem, from roses that tend to flower in clusters. Some of the grandifloras and hybrid teas make large flowers in such tight clusters, none can open properly and fully develop. This is avoided by disbudding, removing all but the dominant, central flower bud from a developing cluster.

Energy is being diverted from the primary flower bud at the tip into the two on either side. Removing the side shoots (disbudding) concentrates the plant's forces and makes the remaining flower larger and stronger.

Cutting flowers to bring indoors is probably the most important summer pruning. The rule is to cut just above an outward facing leaf with 5 leaflets. (To see the difference between a leaflet and a leaf, see page 9). Cutting at this point allows the plant to quickly develop a new flower from the same stem, and the bush will remain attractive.

Rose leaves are compound, meaning divided into leaflets. There is always an odd number of leaflets to one leaf. Close to the flower, leaves will have 1 or 3 leaflets. The first leaf with 5 leaflets will be about halfway down the flower stem. The growth that resumes from this point will have optimum strength to make the best flower. Cut higher and there will be weaker stem growth and smaller flowers.

Dead heading is the prompt removal of flowers as soon as they begin to fade. It directs the energy of the rose towards developing another flower instead of ripening seeds. At the same time, remove twiggy shoots growing into the center of the bush.

Winter Protection

Throughout the South and West even the most tender hybrid tea will survive winter with no special protection. In most of the United States, particularly those areas near the coast, tender roses will survive winter with a minimum of extra care. Hardiness is subject to local variables. On low ground subject to late spring frosts, and in exposed places open to sweeping winds, roses will require more protection than on high, sheltered ground.

Wherever winter temperatures reach zero some degree of winter protection will be necessary. In some areas, the average winter temperature may be relatively high, but can suddenly fall to several degrees below zero. The greatest danger in these areas of sudden severe cold, light snowfalls and strong wind and sleet storms comes in the spring. Many times plants have been induced by a period of warm weather to produce new growth, only to be frozen to the ground shortly thereafter. In these sections of the country, protection should be removed only when spring has arrived convincingly. In the far north where winter temperatures are more severe, the arrival of spring is more certain.

Freezing is a drying process and many roses are more damaged from drying than from cold damage. Before any kind of protection is in place, be sure the soil is thoroughly wet. Antidesiccant sprays also help prevent drying.

There are many ways to protect roses. The best way often varies with the specific region. Some growers actually dig up their roses in fall, bury them under mounds of soil and replant each spring. Others cover their bushes with 6 or 7 inches of soil in fall. When the first freeze comes, they cover the soil with a layer of leaves held in place with wire netting, evergreen branches or similar light material. Others make a cylinder of thin fiber glass, heavy tarpaper or similar material than can fit over the entire bush. Then they fill the cylinder with a loose mulch to insulate the rose.

Whichever method you use, don't start too early. Wait for a hard, killing frost, usually after the temperature has dropped to 13° to 18° F (−18° to −8°C) for several nights.

Comments about winter protection for specific kinds of roses are included in the encyclopedia descriptions in this book.

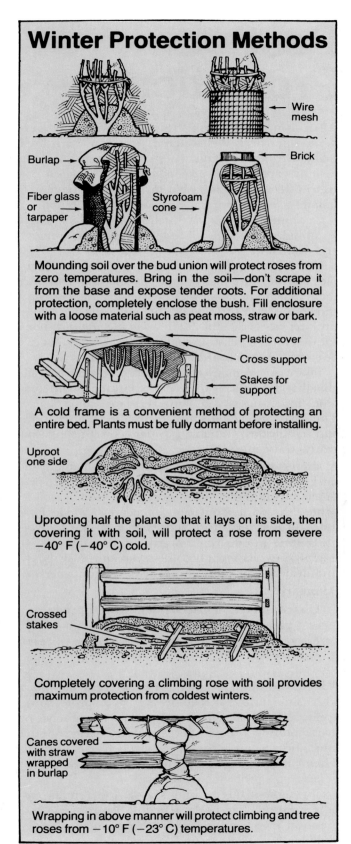

Winter Protection Methods

Wire mesh

Burlap

Brick

Fiber glass or tarpaper

Styrofoam cone

Mounding soil over the bud union will protect roses from zero temperatures. Bring in the soil—don't scrape it from the base and expose tender roots. For additional protection, completely enclose the bush. Fill enclosure with a loose material such as peat moss, straw or bark.

Plastic cover

Cross support

Stakes for support

A cold frame is a convenient method of protecting an entire bed. Plants must be fully dormant before installing.

Uproot one side

Uprooting half the plant so that it lays on its side, then covering it with soil, will protect a rose from severe −40° F (−40° C) cold.

Crossed stakes

Completely covering a climbing rose with soil provides maximum protection from coldest winters.

Canes covered with straw wrapped in burlap

Wrapping in above manner will protect climbing and tree roses from −10° F (−23° C) temperatures.

Pest Protection

All rose protection programs begin with good gardening practices. Well watered, pruned and fertilized plants are most resistant to pests. Other steps towards a healthy garden involve keeping the garden clean and free of weeds. Weeds harbor many kinds of pests, and fallen leaves and prunings are sources of infection.

Examine your plants frequently. As soon as you find an aphid or blackspot infected leaf or twig, remove and destroy it.

The following protection programs are good examples but there are many other possible variations. Use them as a guide, along with the specific pest remedies shown in the illustration on the opposite page. Study product labels carefully. They will include directions for use, as well as listing companion products that can be combined in a coordinated program.

There are so many rose protection products available that it is possible to become confused. Some combine insecticides and fertilizers for convenience. There are also liquid sprays of fertilizers, insecticides and fungicides; wettable powders for spraying and ready-to-use dusts.

A simple program—Begin with a combination product. A dry fertilizer-insecticide product applied 3 or 4 times during the growing season will feed as well as protect the plants from many insect pests. Add to this a lime sulfur spray before buds swell in spring and you have gone a long way towards protecting roses. If mildew and blackspot become severe, it is easy to rely on sulfur or folpet dusts in ready-to-use containers.

Summary:

1. **Use combination insecticide-fertilizer products 3 or 4 times per season.**
2. **Rely on dusts to control insect and disease outbreaks.**

A more thorough program for larger gardens—Start with a lime sulfur spray before any winter protection is applied. This will significantly reduce the number of overwintering fungus spores and insect eggs. Spray lime sulfur again in the spring just before buds swell. Then your roses can enter the growing season as free of last year's problems as possible.

Throughout the growing season, use a multi-purpose spray on a 7 to 10-day schedule. For rose diseases, the most effective fungicides are a mixture of folpet and benomyl together, or Triforine, the ingredient in Ortho's Funginex spray. Applied regularly, either will prevent or control most serious diseases of roses.

To control insect pests, use insecticides such as Isotox or Orthene. Either can be added to the fungicides listed previously so that one spray protects roses from both diseases and insects.

Control thrips with a light, misting spray containing Orthene. Because the thrips are in the flowers only, apply the spray to only the buds and flowers.

The specific miticides Karathane and Plictran are effective against mites. Karathane is also an ingredient of Isotox.

Summary:

1. **Feed monthly with the most convenient, practical and economical fertilizer.**
2. **Make two dormant sprays of lime sulfur. The first is in the fall; second in the spring.**
3. **Use fungicide and insecticide sprays every 7 to 10 days.**

SPRAYING

The least expensive and perhaps most convenient sprayer is the hose-end variety. Available from several manufacturers, these simply thread to the end of your hose and siphon partially diluted materials from an attached container. Accuracy is a problem. Actual application rates may vary considerably. These sprayers will use much more pesticide to cover a given number of roses.

A one-gallon plastic tank-type sprayer (or metal tank-types) costs more but is more economical in the long run since it will use much less spray than the hose end sprayer. Such a sprayer is also considerably more accurate.

NOTE: Never spray on a hot or windy day or when the plants need water. Do a thorough job being sure to spray leaf undersides.

DUSTING

Dusts are one of the oldest forms of plant protection materials. They remain the favored approach of many rose gardeners because they require no mixing.

There are many ways to apply dusts. Gardeners of past generations would make a cheesecloth bag two or three layers thick, fill it with a dust, then lightly shake the bag over the plants. Today dust applicators may be gasoline powered blowers, hand cranked blowers, or simple plastic squeeze tubes.

The best applicators make it easy to do a good job of applying a thin, even layer of dust over the leaves. If the leaves become heavily coated with dust, shake the plant so that the excess will fall off.

JAPANESE BEETLE

Unknown west of the Rockies, this is the most damaging of all the beetles that feed on roses. You can kill these pests with milky spore disease. Use lures and traps specifically designed for Japanese beetle. Pick them or knock off into a can.

THRIPS

Minute, nearly invisible pests colonize on flowers and developing buds, especially white flowers. Don't waste spray on leaves. Use Orthene.

APHIDS

Ubiquitous pests most common in spring clustered on soft new growth. Rub or wash off with your hand or rag. Wash off with a strong spray of water. Make a spray of 1 teaspoon mild dishwashing soap per gallon of water. Many insecticides are effective.

POWDERY MILDEW

A serious problem where blackspot isn't. Water in morning, do not wet leaves. Do not over-fertilize. Use Triforine, Actidione PM, Parnon or sulfur to control.

RUST

Fungus disease that causes rust-colored spots on leaf undersides. Most prevalent in California and areas of similar climate. Use Plantvax, Triforine or zineb.

SPIDER MITE

Dot-sized, spider-like pests colonize and make webs on leaf undersides. Use dormant oil sprays. During growing season, use miticide containing Karathane or Plictran.

BLACKSPOT

A serious problem in all areas with summer rains and warm temperatures. Spreads fast, appearing on lower leaves first. Check for resistant varieties; Use benomyl, folpet, Triforine or maneb every 7 days from first pruning to frost.

LEAFHOPPER

Small, hopping insects suck plant juices much as aphids. May transmit virus disease. Use soil-applied systemics or pyrethrum.

ROSE GALL

One of many kinds of galls caused by harmless wasps. Prune to remove.

ROSE SCALES

These pests colonize canes and are largely immobile, hardly seeming alive. They suck plant juices causing a general weakening. Use a dormant oil spray. During growing season, use soil-applied systemics or Orthene.

CROWN GALL

Not common but easily identified by presence of gall. Cut away infected parts if possible. If roots or crown are infected, destroy plant.

NEMATODES

Microscopic worms parasitize roots causing poor growth. If upon root examination, roots are heavily colonized, destroy plants and start a new rose garden in another area. Consult with county extension agent.

Choosing a Rose

There are many reasons for growing roses, and selecting the rose that's right for you should not be difficult. This chapter is dedicated to helping you find and buy the rose you want.

Most of us usually look for color first—whether it's our neighbor's plant, or a photograph printed on a box or in a book. There is nothing wrong with this, of course, but it is wise to look a little further. Will the plant thrive and produce with the care you will give it?

Time of purchase is important. Roses are in full flower and foliage spring through summer or fall. But most roses are sold in late winter in bare-root form when there is no flower or foliage to compare. There are plenty of good reasons for this marketing method, but if you find it the least bit intimidating, simply *wait* until spring. Nurseries have plenty of good roses flowering in containers at that time.

Seeing and smelling roses in a garden situation is very helpful. There are well maintained public rose gardens in most areas. Many have the newest roses on display. There is a list of public rose gardens on page 158. A visit to one of these can be helpful in making your rose choices.

The encyclopedia section of this book beginning on page 67 is one of the most up-to-date guides for choosing roses. They can be purchased at local suppliers or through mail order nurseries such as those on page 53.

Throughout your investigations, be sure to keep an open mind. Encyclopedias by their nature sound very authoritative and absolute. But read on here about how colors can vary widely and fragrance can be strong one day and nonexistent the next. A picture may show a many-petaled, fully double flower, but in your garden it may first appear as a single.

Ratings by the American Rose Society are an excellent guide, but don't automatically disregard a low-rated rose. It may excel in your garden, or have a special virtue that you seek.

Roses are living creatures and a variable lot at that. But roses, of all flowers, will return your efforts many times over. They have been doing so for centuries.

Ken and Christine Pierson of El Cajon, California, have been growing roses for only two years. But they've already accumulated about 200 varieties and have won several awards from their local rose society.

How to Choose a Rose

As we have discussed, there are many ways to choose a rose. If you have read every word up to this point, you can understand the many variables. Roses are of course alive and not easily categorized and standardized.

Rose lists—One of the best ways to choose a rose is by the use you intend for it. Do you want roses for cut flowers or to perform a landscape function? Is it most important the the rose be fragrant or easy to grow? The lists of roses on page 54 are helpful guides for choosing a rose.

Color index—Most roses are chosen on the basis of color. Flower color is the dominant feature of roses and for most of us the most compelling. Use the Color Index beginning on page 58 to easily compare colors and see the wide variety from which you may choose.

Encyclopedia—The encyclopedia in this book includes more than 200 widely available roses of all kinds—hybrid teas, floribundas, grandifloras, climbers, miniatures and shrubs. Organized by class, each is fairly and succinctly described. Within some limits, members of a class share certain characteristics that may require you to restrict your choice to one class or another.

MAKE A LIST

Once you get the hang of it, choosing a rose is a simple and exciting process. But if the thought of selecting one appealing rose over another worries you, make a list. Then search through the descriptions and lists that follow on pages 54 to 57 until one or more meet your requirements. For instance, you want a rose that is a shade of yellow, fragrant and resistant to pests. You want it to be low growing and would like it to serve as a low hedge. Cut flowers would be nice, but are not required. One rose that fits such a check list is 'Spanish Sun'. Others may fit as well. The choice is yours! Here is a sample list.

Name *Spanish Sun*
Landscape use *Hedge*
Rose Class *Floribunda*
Color *Golden yellow*
Plant Form & Foliage *Low and bushy*
Fragrance *Strong. Fruity.*
Special Characteristics *Hardy
Disease Resistant*

Grading Bare-root Roses

All roses sold bare root are graded according to the number and length of their canes. There are three grades which are the same for hybrid teas and grandifloras.

Floribundas are allowed to have shorter canes while climbers need to be slightly longer. Miniatures are not sold bare root. There are three grades:

#1 is the best quality and must have three vigorous, fresh, moist canes at least 18 inches long.

#1-1/2 requires two 15-inch canes.

#2 needs only two 12-inch canes and is generally not recommended.

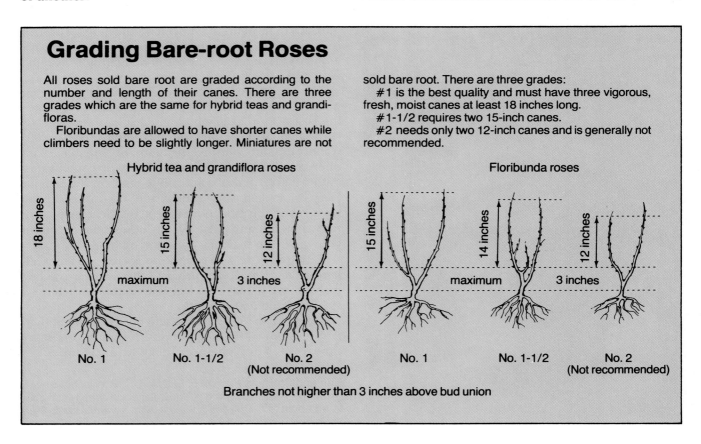

Hybrid tea and grandiflora roses

18 inches · No. 1 · maximum
15 inches · No. 1-1/2 · 3 inches
12 inches · No. 2 (Not recommended)

Floribunda roses

15 inches · No. 1 · maximum
14 inches · No. 1-1/2 · 3 inches
12 inches · No. 2 (Not recommended)

Branches not higher than 3 inches above bud union

WHERE TO BUY

Local nurseries and mail order are the two most common sources of roses. Nurseries usually stock varieties that do particularly well in their area. There you will be able to see and choose the specific plant you want. Many nurseries will replace roses that do poorly despite proper treatment. Nursery personnel can also provide advice as you require.

On the other hand, a larger selection of roses is usually available through mail order (see page 53). Supermarkets and garden departments of department stores also offer roses during rose planting time.

WHEN TO BUY

The best time to buy roses is in late winter or early spring—before spring growth starts. This is the bare-root season and local nurseries will be well supplied.

Most nurseries keep some roses in stock throughout summer. These are planted in containers and cost more. If you use mail order, you can place your order anytime. Mail order companies generally ship at the optimum planting time for your area.

RATING ROSES

Legally, a new rose need be only "distinct" and "new" before it is patented and marketed. The law does not require a rose be particularly worthy or better than others of its kind. For that purpose, the following rating methods were invented. They are the buyer's best guide.

All-America Rose Selections: AARS—Established by leading growers in 1938, AARS is a system of testing new varieties for a two-year period under widely varied soil and climate conditions. George E. Rose, Director of AARS, writes of his organization: "There are 25 official AARS Test Gardens situated throughout the United States. Most are located at universities, or the larger public rose gardens. Most have been functioning for many years. Test gardens are under the rigid supervision of the AARS Test Garden Committee. Specific instructions regarding the layout of the garden, planting, care, time and manner of judging must be followed to the letter."

During the two-year trial period, judges submit four sets of scores. A rose is rated "poor," "fair," "good," "very good" or "excellent" in each of 14 different categories. The categories are: novelty, bud form, flower form, color opening, color finishing, substance, fragrance, stem/cluster, habit, vigor/renewal, foliage, disease resistance, flowering effect and overall value.

Voting by the membership occurs in January by secret ballot. The first rose considered for the award is the one that has received the highest overall two-year score.

One great service of AARS is the annual shipment of the newest roses to AARS-approved public rose gardens throughout the United States. The plants are distributed the season preceding catalog listing, so they may be seen during the blooming season the year they become available. See page 158.

ARS Ratings—Each year, members of the American Rose Society rate the new roses. Roses to be evaluated are listed in a spring issue of *The American Rose* magazine. Rose growers of all kinds, from the most sophisticated to beginners, vote on a scale of one to ten. Their votes are received by a district coordinator who computes an average and distills voters' additional comments into a pithy assessment of the rose variety. The results of each district are published in the *American Rose Annual*. After a rose is used commercially for five years, a national average rating is established.

These ratings, also called Proof of the Pudding, are the best guides for you to follow when making a choice. Note that the ARS rating is listed for each rose in the encyclopedia, unless the rose is too new to be rated. Keep in mind that these ratings, good guides that they are, show an average. It is possible for a rose to have a relatively low rating and still remain in demand. Perhaps it has a unique color, fragrance or offers some other single virtue, though with admitted faults. Or perhaps it excels in some sections of the country, but not in most.

Here's how the ARS rose ratings break down:

10	Perfect
9.9 - 9.0	Superior
8.9 - 8.0	Very Good
7.9 - 7.0	Good
6.9 - 6.0	Average
5.9 - 5.0	Poor
4.9	Very Poor

An Award for Miniatures—The American Rose Society, hybridizers and commercial growers realized that miniature roses could not be judged on the same merits as the full-size garden roses. They are sold in pots, not bare root; most are available in nurseries throughout the year instead of mainly at bare-root time. Because of these differences, the ARS now sponsors an award especially for miniatures—the American Rose Society Award of Excellence for Miniature Roses, or ARSAE.

Gold certificate—The National Gold Medal Certificate has been awarded by the American Rose Society only 13 times in 30 years. It is awarded to rose varieties of any class that have given the best performance over a period of five years. The recipients are 'Peace', 'City of York', 'Carrousel', 'Fashion', 'Frensham', 'Vogue', 'Chrysler Imperial', 'Golden Wings', 'Queen Elizabeth', 'Montezuma', 'Spartan', 'Tropicana' and 'Toy Clown'.

The floribunda, 'Simplicity' in three stages of bloom.

Buds and Flowers

Each rose listed in the encyclopedia includes a description of bud and flower shape. Actually, the descriptions of the shapes are quite variable. Roses are more "a little of this" or "a bit of that". However, the American Rose Society has established groups of basic bud and flower shapes.

Technically, according to the ARS, a *bud* is "in full color and not more than one-fourth to one-third open." It becomes a *bloom* upon opening more than half-way.

BUDS MAY BE:

Slender or tapered—These gradually expand from the base to the center, then taper toward the top at about the same degree as toward the base. 'Blue Moon' is an example.

Pointed—More fully expanded at the base, the bud tapers to a distinct point at the top. 'Charlotte Armstrong' is an example.

Ovoid—Sometimes called *egg-shaped,* this bud has a full base that narrows to a basically rounded end. 'Peace' is an example.

Urn-shaped—The bud is rounded at the base, narrows near the top, then widens at the tip. 'Pink Parfait' has this type bud.

Rounded—Also called *globular,* these are simply round. The lower half forms an almost perfect semicircle. An example is 'Red Devil'.

FLOWERS MAY BE:

Pointed and high centered—This is the classic rose flower shape. It attracts the most attention and affection. 'Century Two' and 'Christian Dior' are good examples.

Globular and globular high centered—The shape of this flower is nearly round, particularly toward the base. Examples are 'Queen Elizabeth' or 'Peace'.

Cupped—The outer shape of the bloom is like a cup in profile. 'Gypsy' has this shape flower.

Flat or thin—This flower is not deep. Petals extend at nearly right angles from the flower base. 'Sterling Silver' is an example.

Camellia-like or imbricated—This form is characteristic only of fully open blooms. The petals are successively bent back over each other like a camellia.

Informal or cactus—The petals of such flowers are not uniform, giving the flower an irregular outline. Some of the older species roses have this type flower.

FLOWERS

All wild roses and some modern ones bear flowers that have only five petals. This is the rose's natural complement of petals and so it is called *single.* Roses that have as many as 15 petals are called *semidouble.* If more than 15, the flowers are called *fully double.* Rose books sound absolute: "35 to 40 petals: Fully double." But again, "It depends." Weather is the main influence. When temperatures are cool, buds grow for a long time before opening. Flowers then will have more than the average number of petals. During the hottest days of summer, buds grow fast and water and nutrients may be in short supply. Flowers then will frequently have fewer and perhaps many fewer petals than average. Conversely, cool weather often makes problems for many-petaled flowers. Roses with 55 to 60 petals may clump-up or "ball" instead of opening properly. If your area frequently has cool and damp weather, such as along a coast, flowers with 50 or fewer petals will perform better.

Substance is the amount of moisture and starch in the petals. It is the quantity and quality of matter in the petals. It determines texture, crispness, firmness, thickness and toughness. Good substance improves the stability and durability of form and the keeping quality of the rose. Red roses with good substance appear velvety; pastels appear opalescent. Yellows and whites have a sparkle and sheen.

Remontant flowering is a term that means continual flowering, a quality much desired by hybridizers. All modern hybrid teas, grandifloras, floribundas and miniatures are remontant to greater and lesser degrees. Remontant roses produce a flower at the end of almost every new shoot.

Some climbers and most of the wild and old roses do not flower at shoot tips. They make flowers on laterals that develop from new shoots, and have only one blooming period a year, usually in spring.

Basic Bud Forms

Tapered   Pointed   Ovoid   Urn-shaped   Rounded

Basic Flower Forms

Pointed/high centered   Globular/high centered   Cupped   Flat

Number of Petals

Single: 5 petals   Semidouble: 5 to 15 petals   Double: 15 and more petals

These photographs of the miniature rose, 'Puppy Love', demonstrate how rose color can vary according to heat and light intensity. 'Puppy Love', above, was photographed in spring at Portland, Oregon, and, below, in midsummer at San Jose, California.

Color

It is the color of a rose that, without warning, takes your breath away. Color is the source of first attraction to a rose and the most important basis on which most of us choose a rose.

Rose color is not nearly as certain as you might imagine. Even though a catalog (or even this book!) says a particular rose is "flame orange," its first flower in your garden may be pale pink.

Photographs, in the case of rose color, can also mislead. A photograph only shows a particular rose in a particular garden at a particular time of day. The same rose photographed at three-hour intervals in a single day may look like three different roses. The makers of this book have worked closely with Consulting Rosarians, hoping to prevent showing a rose with an unnatural color. The photographers have used only natural light to illuminate their subjects.

The color of a rose is a delicate, variable thing. Living pigments responsible for colors in the thin petal membranes are affected by cultural treatments and by all elements of weather—primarily heat and light intensity.

"Fresh," "brilliant," "clear" and "pure" are words used to describe rose colors. A *fresh* color is not diminished by aging, fading, intense light, heat or cold. A *brilliant* rose is radiant and lustrous. Both freshness and brilliance of color will be affected by loss of moisture or substance. A color that is *clear* appears almost translucent. A *pure* color is fresh and clear, clean of spray and dust residue. There are no streaks, spots or blotches of another pigment.

Light intensity is especially important for coral, flame, apricot, peach and multicolors. Roses of these colors are usually derived from a species of rose (*R. foetida*) native to high elevations where light is intense and the air relatively cool. Within the elevations and climates where most of us live, spring is longer (with many cloudy days) and summer is warmer. That is why roses of this heritage tend to be pale in spring when light intensity is low. During midsummer, colors are more intense but tend to fade rapidly because of the high heat. Such roses may benefit from shading during the hottest hours.

Many of our best yellows are derived from the old-fashioned tea roses. They usually reach peak coloration when grown in reduced levels of light intensity.

Red roses are most typically affected by differences in moisture supply and humidity. High humidity and moist soil cause red roses to darken; hence, a red rose may be almost black-red in spring, and a mix of shades ranging all the way to pink in midsummer.

Descriptions of colors need interpretation. For

instance, when the descriptions say "fades in heat," the characteristics discussed previously are evidenced. But fading is not always disagreeable. What if it fades from a respectable orange to a lovely, pale pink-white? Don't ask a rose to fit the book description exactly.

Nutrition and water supply are important in the development of color. Two identical roses in the same garden can make flowers of two different colors. This is especially true if one is well fed, well watered and given a bit of afternoon shade, while the other is ignored and receives full sun all day.

How to choose color—Naturally a book such as this gives you a head start—just look at the photographs. A local nurseryman is always a good information source. If questions persist, check with a local chapter of the American Rose Society. Its members usually know how a particular rose colors in your area.

Fragrance

Watch a friend admire a rose. He examines it first from one angle, then another. He moves in a little closer. Inevitably there is the stoop forward that allows the nose to reach in. The strong, sublime fragrance of "rose" lingers. Does it immediately improve our spirits, or just seem to?

Alice Morse Earle wrote the following many years ago about rose fragrance: "The fragrance of the sweetest rose is beyond any other flower scent, it is irresistible, enthralling; you cannot leave it. I have never doubted the rose has some compelling quality not shared by other flowers. I do not know whether it comes from some inherent witchery of the plant, but it certainly exists."

There is always talk that modern roses have less fragrance. For the most part this criticism is unfair, but there is a bit of truth to it. Hybridizers have worked diligently and scientifically for the last generation to develop the full color potentials of the rose, and have been hugely successful. Roses today are available in a spectrum and variety unimaginable to our ancestors. And, it seems, pleasure to the eye is primary. E.B. Le Grice, in *Rose Growing Complete,* says, "The most vociferous exponent of perfume will forget this quality for the moment when face-to-face with an outstanding color." Bertram Park says in *The Guide to Roses,* "The customer arrives insisting every rose he buys be fragrant. But out among the roses, he is entranced by the glorious show of color . . . Fragrance is forgotten . . ."

Dr. James Alexander Gamble of England agreed that colors and growth habits should be improved, and

Beauty of color and form can be appreciated from a distance, but on closer inspection a rose is sweetly fragrant as well.

the number of varieties increased. But he was a rosarian devoted to rose fragrance. He realized that the variety and depth of rose perfumes could be improved and developed by hybridizers.

To encourage development, Dr. Gamble bequeathed $25,000 to the American Rose Society to support research on the inheritance of fragrance. This would also award hybridizers who produce new roses of outstanding merit—ARS rating of 8.0 or above—that are also "strongly and delightfully fragrant."

Periodically, a special Rose Fragrance Committee is assigned the responsibility of screening new roses and rewarding those that are the most fragrant. The Award is called The James Alexander Gamble Award for Fragrant Roses, and has only been given seven times. If you are looking for a modern rose that has proven itself as a garden rose and is intensely fragrant, look for winners of this award. The seven are: 'Crimson Glory', 'Tiffany', 'Chrysler Imperial', 'Sutter's Gold', 'Granada', 'Fragrant Cloud' and 'Papa Meilland'.

The damask rose—There are many distinct rose fragrances; experts figure about 25 in all. Most of the hybrid teas have one of these seven: rose, nasturtium, orris (iris root extract), violet, apple, lemon and clove. "Rose" fragrance begins with the damask rose—originally from Damascus, capital of Syria, one of the oldest cities of the world.

The damask rose is hardy and can be grown throughout the United States. They are red roses of about 30 petals that normally flower once each spring.

The variety called 'Kazanlik' is the source of much of the world's *attar of rose*. Attar of rose is oil from rose petals that contains the essence of rose perfume. The oil extracted from 32,000 rose flowers is needed to produce one ounce of rose attar. Attar of rose has the consistency of butter and is never a liquid. It may be green, golden or rose colored. The musk rose and cabbage rose are also used to make rose attar.

When roses are most fragrant—Color and fragrance are related. The damask odor is found mainly in the red and pink roses. The fragrance is heavy and does not readily rise from the petals in damp, cool weather. Some heat is required, such as from a sunny day, before the richest, fullest odor is released.

Perfumes of white and yellow roses tend to fall within the nasturtium-orris-violet-lemon range. They are best sniffed during a warm morning; their fragrance is light and may dissipate completely by late afternoon.

Although cool, cloudy days will discourage most fragrant roses, they have no effect on 'Sutter's Gold' and 'Chrysler Imperial'. These are two of the most consistently aromatic roses.

Mildew afflicted roses will have significantly reduced perfume.

Form and Foliage

You will probably want to choose a rose plant from the class that best suits your needs—a hybrid tea, floribunda, grandiflora, miniature, shrub or climber. These classes are based largely upon growth habits (see pages 10 and 11). A sprawling miniature may be a ground cover if planted *en masse;* floribundas generally make excellent landscape shrubs; and climbers can cover an arbor or can be pegged to the ground for a mounding ground cover. For the most part, class will dictate use.

As you might expect, there are differences within a class. 'Sterling Silver' and 'Tiffany' are both low growing hybrid teas, rarely reaching higher than 3 or 4 feet. 'Friendship,' on the other hand, may quite naturally grow to a height of 7 feet. This will have a considerable bearing on your pruning habits, as it would be unnatural to prune all hybrid teas to the same height, regardless of their natural size.

The form of hybrid teas also varies in the degree of upright versus spreading growth. Most vertical growing kinds will become a' narrow tangle unless the interior is periodically cleared and canes are pruned to outward facing buds. Others will be very wide spreading and the opposite treatment will be necessary. This kind of information is noted in the encyclopedia when known. In any case, the plant will reveal its form.

There are many kinds of rose leaves. They may be leathery, exceptionally glossy, more copper-colored when new and so on. The leaves of some of the shrub roses, notably the sweetbriar, *Rosa eglanteria*, common throughout most of the Northwest, are very fragrant.

Leaves of the hybrid tea, 'Peace'.

Roses by Mail

Mail order is often the only source of some hard-to-find roses. Many of the following nurseries are specialists. Their catalogs are in themselves an education. Telephone numbers are listed if the nursery takes calls.

Jackson & Perkins Co.
83A Rose Lane
Medford, OR 97501
(503) 776-2121
Largest rose grower in the world, more than 16 million roses growing at any one time. Official AARS demonstration garden open to public. Free, 32-page color catalog primarily lists roses, but also includes bulbs, vegetables, perennials, berries and dwarf fruit trees.

Kelly Bros. Nurseries, Inc.
650 Maple St.
Dansville, NY 14437
(716) 335-2211
Free, 70-page color catalog offers a wide range of nursery stock, including complete listings of miniatures, hybrid teas, floribundas and grandifloras.

McDaniel's Miniature Roses
7523 Zemco St.
Lemon Grove, CA 92045
(619) 469-4669
Free listing of many varieties of miniature roses includes cultural information. Plants shipped air mail year-round. Many unusual varieties can be supplied—write with your requests.

Miniature Plant Kingdom
Don and Becky Herzog
4125 Harrison Grade Road
Sebastopol, CA 95472
(707) 874-2233
Catalog $1 (refundable). Over 700 varieties. Open 9 a.m. to 4 p.m. Thursday through Sunday; Monday and Tuesday by appointment.

Mini-Roses
Ernest D. Williams
Box 4255, Station A
Dallas, TX 75208
Free, 16-page catalog; spring mailer sent May 1 announces new varieties. "Foremost breeder of hybrid tea form miniature roses."

Nor'East Miniature Roses, Inc.
Harm, Chip and John Saville
58 Hammond St.
Rowley, MA 01969
(617) 948-2408
also
Nor'East Miniature Roses, Inc.
P.O. Box 473
Ontario, CA 91762
(714) 988-7222
Beautiful, 18-page color catalog of many unusual varieties, including most Award of Excellence miniature roses. Official AARS demonstration garden.

Pixie Treasures
4121 Prospect Ave.
Yorba Linda, CA 92686
(714) 993-6780
Descriptive 15-page catalog ($1, refundable on first order) includes 200 of the "finest and latest varieties" of miniature roses. Company is family owned and operated. Plants are guaranteed healthy on arrival.

Rosehill Farm
Gregg Neck Road, Box 406
Galena, MD 21635
(301) 648-5538
Free color catalog features only miniature roses. Shipped year-round with 60-day guarantee. Retail and wholesale. Mastercard and Visa accepted.

Roses by Fred Edmunds, Inc.
6235 S.W. Kahle Road
Wilsonville, OR 97070
Color 32-page catalog free upon request. Many types and varieties of roses, including some of foreign introduction. All are guaranteed.

Roses of Yesterday and Today
(formerly Tillotson's Roses)
802 Brown Valley Road
Watsonville, CA 95076
(408) 724-3537
Informative 70-page catalog costs $2. Specialty is old, rare and unusual roses, many of historical importance. Also many new, hardy shrub roses. Visa and Mastercard accepted.

Sequoia Nursery
Moore Miniature Roses
2519 E. Noble
Visalia, CA 93277
Free color catalog in spring and fall features varieties hybridized by Ralph Moore. Wholesale and retail mail orders accepted. Many novelty miniatures, bush varieties, hanging baskets and miniature tree roses, some with lavender, orange and striped flowers.

Stocking Rose Nursery
785 N. Capitol Ave.
San Jose, CA 95133
(408) 258-3606
Free, 28-page color catalog offers good selection of hybrid teas, grandifloras, floribundas, climbing and tree roses. Many AARS award winners. Open 8:30 to 5 daily, 10 to 5 Sundays, closed Thursdays. Official AARS test garden.

Tate Rose Nursery
Route 20, Box 436
Tyler, TX 75708
Free listing includes 100 varieties of popular hybrid teas, floribundas, grandifloras and climbers. Many patented roses. Roses not shipped to California.

Thomasville Nurseries, Inc.
The Hjorts
P.O. Box 7 (Zip) 31799
1842 Smith Ave.
Thomasville, GA 31792
(912) 226-5568
Good selection of many kinds of roses. Descriptive 24-page catalog free upon request. Also lists native and evergreen azaleas, liriope and daylilies. Official AARS test garden open to public from mid-April to mid-November.

Tiny Petals Miniature Roses
489 Minot Ave.
Chula Vista, CA 92010
(619) 422-0385
The largest selection of the 'Cream of the Crop' in miniatures. Open daily. Beautiful garden displays. Blooms year-round. Visitors and garden groups welcome. Free catalog. Plants guaranteed healthy on arrival. Visa and Mastercard accepted.

Rose Lists

The following lists are based on the recommendations of Consulting Rosarians from throughout the United States. In some cases, they recommend roses not included in this book. Please consult with your nurseryman, local rose society or the American Rose Society for additional information.

HIGH-RATED ROSES

Members of the American Rose Society rate roses on a scale ranging between 1 and 10 (page 47). Here are the highest rated roses of various classes.

Hybrid teas

First Prize	9.0
Peace	9.0
Granada	8.9
Tiffany	8.8
Tropicana	8.8
Mister Lincoln	8.7
Garden Party	8.6
Double Delight	8.5
Paradise	8.5
Lady X	8.4

Grandifloras

Queen Elizabeth	9.0
Pink Parfait	8.4
Sonia	8.0
Montezuma	7.7
Olé	7.7
Camelot	7.7
Mount Shasta	7.7
Carrousel	7.6

Floribundas

Europeana	8.8
Little Darling	8.8
Iceberg	8.6
Walko	8.5
Gene Boerner	8.4
Sea Pearl	8.4
Betty Prior	8.3
Floradora	8.3

Miniatures

Starina	9.4
Beauty Secret	9.0
Cinderella	8.9
Toy Clown	8.9
Magic Carrousel	8.9
Judy Fischer	8.8
Mary Marshall	8.7
Simplex	8.6
Starglo	8.6
Chipper	8.5
Holy Toledo	8.5
Over the Rainbow	8.5

Climbers

Altissimo	8.8
Don Juan	8.6
Handel	8.6
Dortmund	8.6
May Queen	8.4
Royal Flush	8.3
Royal Sunset	8.1
America	8.0
Aurora	8.0
Climbing First Prize	8.0

Old roses

Mme Hardy—damask	9.0
Rosa rubrifolia	9.0
Rosa hugonis	9.0
Koenigin von Daenemark—alba	8.9
Sombreuil—tea	8.6
Mme Plantier—alba	8.6
Tuscany—gallica	8.4
Paul's Early Blush—hybrid perpetual	8.3
Rosa damascena bifera—damask	8.2
Vierge de Clery—centifolia	8.2

Shrub roses

Cornelia—hybrid moschata	9.0
Will Scarlet—hybrid moschata	8.8
Ruskin—hybrid rugosa	8.5
Pink Grootendorst—hybrid rugosa	8.5
Alchymist—shrub	8.4
Nevada—hybrid moyesii	8.4
Country Dancer—shrub	8.2
Rosa rugosa rubra	8.2
Sea Foam—shrub	8.1
Mermaid—hybrid bracteata	8.0

'Climbing Handel'

Medal winners of rose shows throughout the United States are reported to the ARS. They are scored according to best of the class, second best of their class, and so on. The following list includes the top 10 exhibition roses for 1973-1982 in four classes. Exhibition roses are also highly rated for use in the home garden.

Top 10 Exhibition Roses for 10-Year Period (1973-1982)

Hybrid Teas	Ranking
First Prize	1
Garden Party	2
Royal Highness	3
Pristine	4
Peace	5
Pascali	6
Double Delight	7
Granada	8
Swarthmore	9
Toro	10

Grandifloras	Ranking
Queen Elizabeth	1
Aquarius	2
Pink Parfait	3
Sonia	4
Montezuma	5
Mount Shasta	6
Camelot	7
Comanche	8
Scarlet Knight	9
Olé	10

Floribundas	Ranking
Europeana	1
Little Darling	2
Gene Boerner	3
Ivory Fashion	4
First Edition	5 (tie)
Iceberg	5 (tie)
Fire King	6
Angel Face	7
Redgold	8
Sea Pearl	9
Vogue	10

Miniatures	Ranking
Starina	1
Magic Carrousel	2
Toy Clown	3
Mary Marshall	4
Beauty Secret	5
Starglo	6
Judy Fischer	7
Rise 'n' Shine	8
Over the Rainbow	9
Cinderella	10

EASY-TO-GROW ROSES

All roses are easy to grow, but some will tolerate more neglect because of their greater vigor or disease resistance. It is a relative measure—many floribundas and shrub roses are very tough. All of these will perform well with a minimum of care.

Aquarius—grandiflora
Bewitched—hybrid tea
Charlotte Armstrong—hybrid tea
Double Delight—hybrid tea
Duet—hybrid tea
Fragrant Cloud—hybrid tea
Granada—hybrid tea
King's Ransom—hybrid tea
Lady X—hybrid tea
Lucky Lady—grandiflora
Peace—hybrid tea
Queen Elizabeth—grandiflora
Simplicity—floribunda

'Aquarius'

LONG-LASTING CUT ROSES

How long a rose will last after cutting depends primarily upon how it is treated. See page 156. All things being equal, thick-petaled roses will last longest. A good rose for cutting should have long stems, so this list is restricted to hybrid teas and grandifloras.

Camelot
Christian Dior
Duet
Electron
Miss All-American Beauty
Montezuma
Olé
Peace
Prominent
Royal Highness
Swarthmore
Tiffany
Tropicana

HOT-WEATHER HYBRID TEAS

Hot weather affects roses two ways: They grow faster, sometimes too fast, and they are stressed. Rose flowers with 50 or more petals often will not open properly in cool weather and do best with plenty of heat. But many good roses just can't produce their full-sized flowers when weather is hot.

Heat-tolerant hybrid teas can be divided into two groups—those recommended for hot and dry climates and those recommended for hot and humid climates. Consultants are the Tucson Rose Society and Gulf Coast Consulting Rosarians Jim Miller and Dr. E.W. Lyle.

Reliable hybrid teas for hot and dry climates:
Charlotte Armstrong
Chrysler Imperial
Double Delight
First Prize
Granada
Miss All-American Beauty
Mister Lincoln
Oldtimer
Peace
Royal Highness
Sutter's Gold
Tropicana

Reliable hybrid teas for hot and humid climates:
Bewitched
Chrysler Imperial
Double Delight
Fragrant Cloud
Garden Party
Honor
Lady X
Mister Lincoln
Paradise
Pascali
Peace
Perfume Delight
Red Masterpiece
Royal Highness
Tiffany
Toro
Tropicana

'Charlotte Armstrong'

COOL-WEATHER HYBRID TEAS

In cool weather growth and bud formation is slow. Flowers with 55 or more petals often cannot grow fast enough to open properly. Petals stick together or ball. Mildew is more of a problem. The following have all won the City of Portland Gold Medal.

Double Delight
Fragrant Cloud
Pascali
Peace
Princess Margret
Prominent
Red Devil

'Garden Party'

COLD WINTER HYBRID TEAS

Wherever winter temperatures drop below zero, most hybrid teas need some winter protection. Where subzero temperatures are the rule, substantial protection will be necessary. Many of the shrub roses are exceptionally hardy and will survive extreme cold with no protection. Floribundas and polyanthas tend to be slightly more cold-tolerant than hybrid teas. The following hybrid teas are recommended by the Northern Chicagoland Rose Society.

Big Ben
Double Delight
First Prize
Fragrant Cloud
Garden Party
Granada
Mister Lincoln
Paradise
Pascali
Peace
Pristine
Sunblest
Swarthmore
Tropicana

FRAGRANT ROSES

These are some of the strongly fragrant roses. Many of the old roses are fragrant. The gallicas are particularly good for *potpourri*. Modern roses that are dark red frequently have the long lasting, old-fashioned perfume. See page 51 for more about rose fragrance. Winners of the James Alexander Gamble Award for Fragrant Roses are noted with an asterisk.

Hybrid teas and grandifloras
Arizona—grandiflora
Chrysler Imperial*—hybrid tea
Command Performance—hybrid tea
Crimson Glory*—hybrid tea
Electron—hybrid tea
Fragrant Cloud*—hybrid tea
Granada*—hybrid tea
Heirloom—hybrid tea
Mister Lincoln—hybrid tea
Oklahoma—hybrid tea
Olé—grandiflora
Papa Meilland*—hybrid tea
Perfume Delight—hybrid tea
Royal Highness—hybrid tea
Sterling Silver—hybrid tea
Sundowner—grandiflora
Sutter's Gold*—hybrid tea
Tiffany*—hybrid tea
Tropicana—hybrid tea
White Lightnin'—grandiflora

'Chrysler Imperial'

Floribundas
Angel Face
Apricot Nectar
Iceberg
Rose Parade
Saratoga
Spanish Sun
Sunsprite

Climbers
America
Blossomtime
Climbing Chrysler Imperial
Climbing Crimson Glory
Climbing Étoile de Hollande
Climbing Peace
Climbing Sutter's Gold
Climbing Tropicana
Don Juan
Red Fountain
Royal Sunset

GROUND COVER ROSES

Many kinds of roses can serve as ground covers. Low-growing floribundas or miniatures can be planted in masses. Some climbers can be "pegged," their long canes pulled back and attached to the ground. Roses classed as ramblers and hybrids of *Rosa sempervirens* have supple, flexible canes and many make excellent ground covers.

Dorothy Perkins—rambler
Evangeline—rambler
Félicité et Perpetue—hybrid sempervirens
Max Graf—hybrid *rugosa*
May Queen—rambler
New Dawn—large-flowered climber
Red Cascade—miniature
Rosa laevigata or Cherokee Rose
Rosa wichuraiana or Memorial Rose
Sea Foam—shrub

'Evangeline' rambler

Pegged climber in bloom.

LOW HEDGE ROSES

Floribundas and polyanthas are naturals here. Low-growing hybrid teas and shrub roses make outstanding low hedges.

Bon-Bon—floribunda
Cathedral—floribunda
Cherish—floribunda
China Doll—polyantha
Country Dancer—shrub
Escapade—floribunda
Europeana—floribunda
First Edition—floribunda
Ginger—floribunda
Iceberg—floribunda
Music Maker—shrub
Sally Holmes—shrub
Sarabande—floribunda
Simplicity—floribunda
Spartan—floribunda
Sunsprite—floribunda
The Fairy—polyantha
Trumpeter—floribunda
Virgo—hybrid tea
Yesterday—floribunda

'Europeana' in front, 'Cathedral' at rear.

LOW EDGING ROSES

Neat, 10-inch edging borders are a particularly effective use for miniature roses. Here are several of the best.

Beauty Secret
Bo Peep
Cinderella
Cricri
Hula Girl
Judy Fischer
Popcorn
Puppy Love
Red Flush
Red Imp
Rise 'n' Shine
Starina
White Angel
Yellow Doll

TALL SHRUB ROSES

There are several varieties to chose between. Many excellent shrubs have come from Kordes in Germany. Professor Buck of Iowa State has developed many low-maintenance shrub roses. Some are species from which our garden roses have derived.

Applejack—shrub
Berlin—shrub
Bonn—shrub
Carefree Beauty—shrub
Elmshorn—shrub
F.J. Grootendorst—hybrid *rugosa*
Fritz Nobis—shrub
Frühlingsgold—hybrid *spinosissima*
Golden Wings—shrub
Mermaid—hybrid *bracteata*
Montezuma—grandiflora
Phyllis Bide—rambler
Queen Elizabeth—grandiflora
Rosa banksiae (yellow or white) Lady
   Banks Rose
Rosa rugosa Japanese Rose
Rosa soulieana
Sitka—shrub
Sparrieshoop—shrub

'Sparrieshoop'

Rosa banksiae normalis

DISEASE-RESISTANT ROSES

No modern rose is immune to all diseases and there are many degrees of "resistance." Climate is the primary influence. Rust is a problem in California and the Southwest where blackspot is rare. Blackspot is a problem in climates with summer rain. A rose may successfully resist blackspot in Los Angeles but be devastated by it in Louisiana. Many of the shrub roses, species roses and polyanthas are more disease resistant than most of the modern roses. Fungicides will effectively control mildew, blackspot and rust.

The following lists are the results of a symposium conducted by Lincoln Atkiss of Newton Square, Pennsylvania. Representatives of public rose gardens throughout the U.S. were questioned and their responses tabulated. They were limited to the hybrid teas, grandifloras and floribundas. Roses are listed in descending order.

Most disease resistant
Tropicana*
Queen Elizabeth
Prominent
Miss All-American Beauty
Pristine
Peace
Tiffany
Cathedral
Fragrant Cloud
Pascali
Pink Peace
Europeana

Hybrid teas most resistant to blackspot
Tropicana*
First Prize
Miss All-American Beauty
Mister Lincoln
Tiffany
Portrait
Pink Peace
Pristine
Proud Land
Duet
Peace
Electron

Grandifloras and floribundas most resistant to blackspot
Queen Elizabeth
Prominent
Rose Parade
Razzle Dazzle
Gene Boerner
Europeana
Montezuma
First Edition
Ivory Fashion
Sonia
Carrousel
Angel Face

Hybrid teas most resistant to mildew
Tiffany
Pristine
Miss All-American Beauty
Futura
Pascali
Peace
Seashell
Pink Peace
Proud Land
Mister Lincoln
Tropicana*
Chicago Peace

Grandifloras and floribundas most resistant to mildew
Queen Elizabeth
Europeana
Rose Parade
Charisma
Sarabande
Saratoga
Cathedral
Sunsprite
Prominent
Razzle Dazzle
First Edition
Evening Star

'First Prize'

*'Tropicana' is very resistant to blackspot, and, throughout most of the United States, mildew. In the western states, it is quite prone to mildew.

'Chicago Peace'

Roses by Color — Red and Lavender

As hybridizers have busily created more and more colors, gardeners have become both entranced and confused. Will the colors clash or will they complement each other? It is true a garden should please you, above all else, but the trick is to know in advance exactly what color combinations will be most pleasing.

Today the American Rose Society officially recognizes 16 distinct color classes. They are: *white or near white, medium yellow, deep yellow, yellow blend, apricot blend, orange and orange blend, orange-red, light pink, medium pink, deep pink, pink blend, medium red, dark red, red blend, mauve* and *russet.* Understandably, many roses do not fit neatly into any of these categories. Russet is rarely seen, and there is a wide range of colors called *orange.*

All the hybrid teas, floribundas and grandifloras described in the encyclopedia are shown on these pages. They are arranged in seven color categories: *red, lavender, pink, yellow, orange, white* and *multicolor.* Degrees of shade, tint and brightness will be apparent in each group. This approach, while not as rigorous as the ARS color classes, enables you to make comparisons. Climbing and miniature roses are treated separately on pages 125 to 147.

You may want to begin your selection process here. The name of each rose, its class and the page on which it is described are noted for your convenience.

Red

Carrousel
Grandiflora   Page 119

Charlotte Armstrong
Hybrid Tea   Page 69

Eutin
Floribunda   Page 103

Eye Paint
Floribunda   Page 104

Gypsy
Hybrid Tea   Page 77

Oklahoma
Hybrid Tea   Page 85

Olé
Grandiflora   Page 121

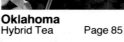

Proud Land
Hybrid Tea   Page 89

Swarthmore
Hybrid Tea   Page 92

Wini Edmunds
Hybrid Tea   Page 95

Lavender

Angel Face
Floribunda   Page 98

Blue Moon
Hybrid Tea   Page 69

Christian Dior
Hybrid Tea   Page 70

Chrysler Imperial
Hybrid Tea   Page 70

Comanche
Grandiflora   Page 119

Crimson Glory
Hybrid Tea   Page 71

Europeana
Floribunda   Page 103

John S. Armstrong
Grandiflora   Page 120

Kentucky Derby
Hybrid Tea   Page 79

Merci
Floribunda   Page 109

Mirandy
Hybrid Tea   Page 82

Mister Lincoln
Hybrid Tea   Page 83

Red Devil
Hybrid Tea   Page 89

Red Masterpiece
Hybrid Tea   Page 89

Red Pinocchio
Floribunda   Page 111

Sarabande
Floribunda   Page 113

Scarlet Knight
Grandiflora   Page 122

Deep Purple
Floribunda   Page 102

Heirloom
Hybrid Tea   Page 77

Lady X
Hybrid Tea   Page 81

Paradise
Hybrid Tea   Page 86

Sterling Silver
Hybrid Tea   Page 91

Roses by Color — Pink

Using color—Ed Kaptur, whose garden is shown on page 28, speaks for many rose gardeners when he says, "Plant a lot of one color." For an effective landscape display, use at least four of the same color hybrid tea. Or use more than four floribundas. Choose a color you like, one that will fit in with your house and garden.

A strong contrast can be pleasing or harsh. A row of the red 'Europeana' in front of taller, white 'Iceberg' or 'Honor' makes an eye-catching color combination. Unless you plant a large number of plants, strong, vibrant colors, especially oranges, are difficult to blend successfully.

The multicolors, pale yellows, whites and creams, will complement surrounding color.

Some rose gardens do not have to blend with the landscape. In the backyard or an out-of-the-way corner, colors may mix or clash at random. For a cutting garden, it may be preferable to include as many colors as possible.

Anabell
Floribunda   Page 98

Aquarius
Grandiflora   Page 118

Betty Prior
Floribunda   Page 99

Cherish
Floribunda   Page 101

China Doll
Floribunda   Page 101

Duet
Hybrid Tea   Page 72

Friendship
Hybrid Tea   Page 75

Gene Boerner
Floribunda   Page 106

Helen Traubel
Hybrid Tea   Page 78

Jadis
Hybrid Tea   Page 80

Miss All-American Bea
Hybrid Tea   Page 83

Queen Elizabeth
Grandiflora   Page 122

Rose Parade
Floribunda   Page 112

Royal Highness
Hybrid Tea   Page 90

Sea Pearl
Floribunda   Page 112

Simplicity
Floribunda   Page 113

Bewitched
Hybrid Tea   Page 68

Bon-Bon
Floribunda   Page 99

Camelot
Grandiflora   Page 119

Cécile Brunner
Polyantha   Page 100

Century Two
Hybrid Tea   Page 69

Eiffel Tower
Hybrid Tea   Page 73

Electron
Hybrid Tea   Page 73

Fashion
Floribunda   Page 104

First Love
Hybrid Tea   Page 74

First Prize
Hybrid Tea   Page 74

Perfume Delight
Hybrid Tea   Page 87

Peter Frankenfield
Hybrid Tea   Page 87

Pink Parfait
Grandiflora   Page 121

Pink Peace
Hybrid Tea   Page 88

Portrait
Hybrid Tea   Page 88

Sonia
Grandiflora   Page 123

Spellbinder
Hybrid Tea   Page 91

The Doctor
Hybrid Tea   Page 93

The Fairy
Polyantha   Page 115

Tiffany
Hybrid Tea   Page 94

Choosing a rose **61**

Roses by Color — Yellow and Orange

Yellow

Buccaneer
Grandiflora   Page 118

Eclipse
Hybrid Tea   Page 72

Irish Gold
Hybrid Tea   Page 78

Katherine Loker
Floribunda   Page 108

Summer Sunshine
Hybrid Tea   Page 91

Sunsprite
Floribunda   Page 114

Orange

Apricot Nectar
Floribunda   Page 98

Bahia
Floribunda   Page 99

First Edition
Floribunda   Page 105

Fragrant Cloud
Hybrid Tea   Page 75

Futura
Hybrid Tea   Page 76

Ginger
Floribunda   Page 105

Gingersnap
Floribunda   Page 106

Montezuma
Grandiflora   Page 120

Oldtimer
Hybrid Tea   Page 85

Orangeade
Floribunda   Page 110

Prominent
Grandiflora   Page 122

Seashell
Hybrid Tea   Page 90

King's Ransom
Hybrid Tea   Page 80

Lemon Spice
Hybrid Tea   Page 81

New Day
Hybrid Tea   Page 84

Oregold
Hybrid Tea   Page 85

Spanish Sun
Floribunda   Page 114

Bing Crosby
Hybrid Tea   Page 68

Cathedral
Floribunda   Page 100

City of Belfast
Floribunda   Page 102

Command Performance
Hybrid Tea   Page 71

Firelight
Hybrid Tea   Page 73

Margo Koster
Polyantha   Page 108

Marina
Floribunda   Page 109

Matador
Floribunda   Page 109

Medallion
Hybrid Tea   Page 82

Mojave
Hybrid Tea   Page 84

Spartan
Floribunda   Page 114

Sundowner
Grandiflora   Page 123

Tropicana
Hybrid Tea   Page 94

Trumpeter
Floribunda   Page 115

Typhoo Tea
Hybrid Tea   Page 94

Roses by Color — White, Bicolor and Multicolor

White

Evening Star
Floribunda Page 104

Garden Party
Hybrid Tea Page 76

Honor
Hybrid Tea Page 78

Iceberg
Floribunda Page 107

Pascali
Hybrid Tea Page 86

Pristine
Hybrid Tea Page 88

Saratoga
Floribunda Page 111

Sweet Afton
Hybrid Tea Page 93

White Lightnin'
Grandiflora Page 123

Chicago Peace
Hybrid Tea Page 70

Circus
Floribunda Page 101

Circus Parade
Floribunda Page 102

Color Magic
Hybrid Tea Page 71

Double Delight
Hybrid Tea Page 72

Lustige
Hybrid Tea Page 82

Peace
Hybrid Tea Page 86

Piccadilly
Hybrid Tea Page 87

Picnic
Floribunda Page 110

Redgold
Floribunda Page 111

Ivory Fashion
Floribunda   Page 107

Ivory Tower
Hybrid Tea   Page 79

John F. Kennedy
Hybrid Tea   Page 79

Misty
Hybrid Tea   Page 84

Mount Shasta
Grandiflora   Page 121

White Masterpiece
Hybrid Tea   Page 95

Bicolor/
Multicolor

American Heritage
Hybrid Tea   Page 68

Arizona
Grandiflora   Page 118

Charisma
Floribunda   Page 100

Forty-Niner
Hybrid Tea   Page 74

Granada
Hybrid Tea   Page 77

Kordes' Perfecta
Hybrid Tea   Page 81

Little Darling
Floribunda   Page 108

Love
Grandiflora   Page 120

Snowfire
Hybrid Tea   Page 90

Sunset Jubilee
Hybrid Tea   Page 92

Sutter's Gold
Hybrid Tea   Page 92

Talisman
Hybrid Tea   Page 93

Yankee Doodle
Hybrid Tea   Page 95

Hybrid Teas

Bright color, elegant form, long stems, vigor—all these words describe the hybrid tea.

Hybrid teas are the great roses of the world. They are grown in beds for a dramatic display of color. They are cultivated by the perfectionist working and waiting for the "perfect" rose flower. They are planted by the romantic who desires an occasional charming red rose. In short, hybrid teas are the modern expression of everything a rose should be.

These are high powered, flower making machines. Their colors are rich—ranging from pure white through fine gradations of pinks and reds to crimson, copper, gold and yellow. Many are fragrant. They produce lots of flowers, from spring until first frost.

Some hybrid teas grow low and spreading, while others become tall. As hybrids, they are of mixed heritage. There is a little of the vigorous and robust hybrid perpetual and some of the more delicate tea rose.

Hybrid teas are a culmination of years of work by plant explorers, hybridizers and gardeners. Imagine the classic roses of Europe blended with the roses of China. Add a dash from the many wild roses and that's the story of the hybrid tea.

La France—The hybrid tea has existed as a class of rose for only 100 years. Until they were developed, the great rose of Europe was the *hybrid perpetual*. In the late 1800's thousands of varieties of this rose were available. The hybrid perpetual could be described as a "mongrel," a mix of all the popular roses grown before it. There were also "tea" roses brought from China in the 1800's. These were more delicate, less understood and grown less often, but they contributed to the grace of the modern hybrid tea.

In 1867, J.B. Guillot crossed hybrid perpetual and tea roses. Thirteen years later, 'La France' was recognized as the first of a new class of roses, subsequently named "hybrid tea."

Soleil d'Or—An important shift in the development of the hybrid tea came with 'Soleil d'Or'. It was the result of crossing a hybrid perpetual and the Persian yellow rose, *Rosa foetida persiana*. Not only were yellows, golds and oranges added, but even the traditional red was improved. The rapid, repeat-blooming characteristic of modern hybrid teas was partially a contribution of the Persian yellow.

'Soleil d'Or' and its immediate descendants were classed as *pernetianas*. All pernetianas shared the qualities of new and brilliant color, early bloom, smooth leaves, thin, straight thorns and, unfortunately, susceptibility to blackspot. The pernetianas survived as a class until about 1930, when their individuality was lost to the greater class of roses known as the hybrid teas.

Proud parents—Some roses make outstanding parents and have the ability to pass along their best characteristics to their offspring. Noteworthy in this respect are the hybrid teas 'Crimson Glory' and 'Charlotte Armstrong'.

'Crimson Glory' appeared first, in 1935, with large, deep crimson flowers of intense fragrance. Five years later a cross of 'Soeur Thérèse' and 'Crimson Glory' produced 'Charlotte Armstrong', which, considered only on the basis of its many high-quality descendents, is one of the most important hybrid teas of all time. Noted progeny include: 'Chrysler Imperial', 'Forty-Niner', 'Helen Traubel', 'Garden Party', 'Mojave', 'Tiffany', 'Mirandy' and 'Sutter's Gold'.

World's favorite—'Peace' is the world's favorite rose according to a recent poll of rose societies from 11 nations. Runner-up was 'Fragrant Cloud', followed by 'Queen Elizabeth' and 'Chrysler Imperial'.

The story of 'Peace' is most remarkable. It begins in France when the Nazi invasion forced young Francis Meilland to smuggle three one-pound packages of an experimental rose into other countries. Two of the packages were confiscated, but the third, sent to Robert Pyle of Conard-Pyle Roses in the United States, arrived. Ten years later, after this rose had been tested throughout the United States, the ARS planned a special name-giving ceremony. This experimental rose of outstanding character and quality had captured the imagination and hearts of rose growers everywhere. At the Pacific Rose Society Exhibition in Pasadena, California, Robert Pyle declared, "We are persuaded that this greatest new rose of our time should be named for the world's greatest desire—Peace." This became the name of Francis Meilland's rose on April 29, 1945—the same day that Berlin fell.

The day the war with Japan ended, 'Peace' was given the ARS All-America Award. A month later, the day the peace treaty was signed with Japan, 'Peace' received the ARS's supreme award, the Gold Medal. Thirty years later, 'Peace' remains the world's favorite.

Future—The hybrid tea will continue to change. New colors in the plum-purple range are expected by some. Breeders continue to seek improved hardiness and disease resistance. Hybrid teas resistant to blackspot disease are now growing in several test gardens. They will continue to improve as long as hybridizers and gardeners strive to attain the perfect rose.

Left: 'Miss All-American Beauty'.

AMERICAN HERITAGE
Hybrid Tea
ARS Rating: 7.0   Introduced: 1965   AARS 1966

Flower: Long, lovely buds become ivory at the base, blending into salmon with dark, almost red edges. Double, 4 to 6 inches with 50 to 60 petals. Long stems.

Fragrance: Slight.

Form and Foliage: Tall and robust. Tends not to spread. Vigorous grower. Large, dark green leaves.

Comments: A free-blooming cross between 'Queen Elizabeth' and 'Yellow Perfection'. Flowers hold well but color varies due to climate. Prefers hot, dry summers. Sometimes susceptible to winter damage, blossom splitting and mildew.

BEWITCHED
Hybrid Tea
ARS Rating: 7.0   Introduced: 1967   AARS 1967

Flower: Beautifully formed, long, pointed buds open slowly into clear pink blooms with exceptionally high centers. Double, 5 to 6 inches with 35 to 40 petals. Long stems.

Fragrance: Strong. Appealing, old-time spicy aroma.

Form and Foliage: Upright, tall and bushy. Vigorous grower. Clean, glossy green leaves.

Comments: A free-flowering and easy-to-grow cross between 'Queen Elizabeth' and 'Tawny Gold'. Popular with beginners and hobbyists. Buds form quickly and open slowly. Disease resistant. Long lasting as a cut flower. Full foliage makes it a good screen hedge or background plant. Needs winter protection in particularly cold climates. Its only serious fault is a tendency to produce curved flower stems.

BING CROSBY
Hybrid Tea
ARS Rating: 6.9   Introduced: 1980   AARS 1981

Flower: Tight, well formed buds open into brilliant persimmon orange blossoms with a fluorescent glow. Blooms tend to pick up a deeper red later in the year. Double, high-centered, 3-1/2 to 4-1/2 inches with 40 to 50 curved petals. Borne on long stems.

Fragrance: Moderate.

Form and Foliage: Medium to tall, well branched and compact. Large, bright green, waxy leaves.

Comments: Very profuse over a long season. Attractive plant. Disease resistant. Good cut flower.

BLUE MOON
ARS Rating: 7.4

Hybrid Tea

Introduced: 1964

Flower: Long, tapering buds open into large, shapely, pure mauve blooms. Double, 3-1/2 to 4-1/2 inches with 35 to 40 petals. Stiff, upright stems.

Fragrance: Strong.

Form and Foliage: Upright, medium to tall. Vigorous grower. Large, leathery, dark green leaves. Few thorns.

Comments: Color holds true throughout bloom period. Warm days and nights encourage flowering. Disease resistant. Good cut flower. Dark colored flowers and foliage are attractive planted in front of light colored objects.

CENTURY TWO
ARS Rating: 8.3

Hybrid Tea

Introduced: 1971

Flower: Large, long, pointed buds open into high-centered, bright pink blooms. Double, 4-1/2 to 5 inches with 25 to 30 petals. Flowers may appear singly or in clusters on long stems.

Fragrance: Moderate.

Form and Foliage: Medium height, bushy and husky. Vigorous grower. Dense, robust, glossy foliage.

Comments: A 'Charlotte Armstrong' and 'Duet' cross which produces prolific, continual blooms. Buds and blooms hold well. Similar in color to 'Charlotte Armstrong' but with more substance; often called 'Improved Charlotte Armstrong'. Clean foliage makes a good hedge plant, but is somewhat susceptible to mildew.

CHARLOTTE ARMSTRONG
ARS Rating: 7.5

Hybrid Tea

Introduced: 1940   AARS 1941

Flower: Long, pointed, blood red buds open into reddish pink blooms. Double, 3 to 4 inches with 30 to 35 petals. Long stems.

Fragrance: Light.

Form and Foliage: Medium to tall and extremely bushy. Very vigorous grower. Dark green, leathery leaves.

Comments: Many of today's popular rose varieties can be traced to this famous cross between 'Soeur Thérése' and 'Crimson Glory'. Beautiful in all stages, it is typically described as: "Magnificent in the garden because of its great vigor, disease resistance and freedom of blooms." Easy to grow. Likes warm weather. Excellent cut flower.

CHICAGO PEACE
ARS Rating: 8.3

Hybrid Tea

Introduced: 1962

Flower: Big, bold blooms are shimmering pink, blended with canary yellow and sometimes copper tones. Double, 5 to 5-1/2 inches with 50 to 60 petals.

Fragrance: Slight.

Form and Foliage: Medium height, upright and bushy. Very vigorous grower. Large, leathery, glossy green leaves.

Comments: A sport of 'Peace' but with more glorious color. Retains all 'Peace' virtues, such as form, foliage and plant shape. Good cut or exhibition flower.

CHRISTIAN DIOR
ARS Rating: 7.7

Hybrid Tea

Introduced: 1958   AARS 1962

Flower: Blood red, long, pointed buds open into high-centered, brilliant red blooms. Double, 4 to 4-1/2 inches with 55 to 60 petals. Long stems.

Fragrance: Slight.

Form and Foliage: Tall, bushy and upright. Vigorous grower. Rich, dark green, glossy foliage.

Comments: Abundant bloomer. Color becomes more intense and vibrant under strong or artificial light. Flowers have outstanding keeping quality on the bush or cut. Leaves tend to mildew.

CHRYSLER IMPERIAL
ARS Rating: 8.3

Hybrid Tea

Introduced: 1952   AARS 1953

Flower: Large, shapely buds open into big, dark crimson flowers. Double, 4-1/2 to 5 inches with 40 to 50 petals. Long, straight stems.

Fragrance: Strong. Rich and spicy; reminiscent of many perfumes. James Alexander Gamble Medal for Fragrant Roses, 1965.

Form and Foliage: Medium height and bushy. Dull, dark green foliage.

Comments: The standard by which many red roses are judged. A 'Charlotte Armstrong' and 'Mirandy' hybrid with exceptional fragrance and flowers. Good exhibition or cut flower. Needs heat for best performance—the rich, red color will not develop in cool climates. Mildew and blind shoots are occasional problems. National Gold Medal Certificate, 1957.

COLOR MAGIC
Hybrid Tea

ARS Rating: 8.0   Introduced: 1978   AARS 1978

Flower: Large, urn-shaped buds are ivory pink with a touch of peach. They quickly open into huge, high-centered, deep pink blooms that nearly darken to red before petals drop. Aptly named—flower color changes every day. Double, 6 to 7 inches with 35 petals. Usually one flower on a long stem.

Fragrance: Light, sweet.

Form and Foliage: Medium to tall and spreading. Vigorous grower. Attractive, glossy green foliage.

Comments: Because of the change of color, it's like having a different rose in your garden every day. Disease resistant. Excellent cut flower and exhibition rose. Needs winter protection in coldest areas.

COMMAND PERFORMANCE
Hybrid Tea

ARS Rating: 7.2   Introduced: 1970   AARS 1971

Flower: Long, tapered buds unfold into star-shaped, flaming orange blooms. High-centered, double, 5 to 6 inches with 15 to 20 petals. Flowers singly or in clusters.

Fragrance: Strong.

Form and Foliage: Tall and upright. Vigorous grower. Leathery green leaves.

Comments: Prolific flower producer. Main attraction is the glowing orange color. Armstrong Nursery calls it "pure enchantment in the home or garden." Blooms may become distorted with warm, humid weather. Less reliable in the Gulf Coast states. Susceptible to mildew.

CRIMSON GLORY
Hybrid Tea

ARS Rating: 7.6   Introduced: 1935

Flower: Lovely, pointed buds open to become urn-shaped, vivid crimson blooms. Large, double with 30 to 35 petals.

Fragrance: Strong. Intense, old-time damask aroma. Once voted most fragrant by ARS. James Alexander Gamble Medal for Fragrant Roses, 1961.

Form and Foliage: Low, bushy and sprawling. Vigorous grower. Attractive, dark green, glossy leaves.

Comments: Until 'Chrysler Imperial' appeared, 'Crimson Glory' was *the* red rose to which all others were compared. One of the parents of 'Charlotte Armstrong'. Continual bloomer. Grows best in warm climates. Good cut flower.

DOUBLE DELIGHT
Hybrid Tea
ARS Rating: 8.5 Introduced: 1977 AARS 1977

Flower: Rose grower Fred Edmunds properly described this well-known bicolor rose as: "an outstanding novelty. Rich cream with bold splashes of strawberry on the outer row of petals." Double, 5 to 6 inches with about 40 petals. Long stems.

Fragrance: Strong. Intense, spicy aroma.

Form and Foliage: Medium height and bushy. Vigorous grower. Dark green, glossy leaves.

Comments: A real crowd-pleaser and national favorite. Its stunning colors change with exposure to sunlight. Very prolific with many repeated blooms. International award winner. Hardy and disease resistant. Excellent cut flower. Top exhibition rose.

DUET
Hybrid Tea
ARS Rating: 8.2 Introduced: 1960 AARS 1961

Flower: Urn-shaped buds open into medium size, bicolor blooms with salmon-pink inside and rose-crimson outside. Double, 4 inches with 30 to 35 wavy petals. Flowers are clustered on long sturdy stems.

Fragrance: Slight.

Form and Foliage: Tall and bushy. Vigorous, strong and sturdy. Dark green, heavily toothed, holly-like foliage.

Comments: Prolific flower producer—nearly always in bloom. Flowers are very long lasting and hold their color well in all types of weather. Fades nicely. Very mildew resistant and easy to grow. Good as a hedge. Outstanding cut flowers at all stages, from bud to full flower.

ECLIPSE
Hybrid Tea
ARS Rating: 6.7 Introduced: 1935

Flower: Long, streamlined, yellow buds open into primrose yellow blooms. Double, 3 to 5 inches with 25 to 30 petals.

Fragrance: Moderate.

Form and Foliage: Medium height, shapely and upright. Vigorous grower. Thick, gray-green leaves.

Comments: An old-time favorite that profusely bears characteristic long, slim buds, and lovely, all-purpose yellow flowers. Disease resistant.

EIFFEL TOWER
ARS Rating: 7.2

Hybrid Tea
Introduced: 1963

Flower: Large, pink, urn-shaped buds slowly open into large, high-centered, medium pink blooms. Double, 3-1/2 to 5 inches with 30 to 40 petals. Flowers are borne singly on long, strong stems.

Fragrance: Strong.

Form and Foliage: Tall and bushy. Very vigorous grower. Foliage is sparse, leathery and semiglossy.

Comments: Long lasting. Almost thornless. Attractive cut flower. Susceptible to rust and mildew.

ELECTRON
ARS Rating: 7.7   Introduced: 1970   AARS 1973

Hybrid Tea

Flower: Long-lasting, deep rose colored buds open slowly to beautifully formed, "electric" or glowing pink blossoms. High-centered, double, with many petals. Medium length stems. Free blooming.

Fragrance: Strong.

Form and Foliage: Small to medium height, full and bushy. Classic, full, bushy, tea rose form. Thick, dark green, closely spaced leaves cover plant to the ground.

Comments: Produces many flowers that hold their beauty for a long time. Extremely hardy in summer heat. Disease resistant. Winner of seven prestigious European awards for rose quality.

FIRELIGHT
ARS Rating: 6.2

Hybrid Tea
Introduced: 1971

Flower: Egg-shaped and pointed buds of dark orange-red produce fluorescent, coral-red blooms. Double, 6 inches with 35 to 40 petals. Long stems.

Fragrance: Moderate. Rich and fruity.

Form and Foliage: Tall, sturdy and vigorous. Light green, leathery leaves.

Comments: Huge flowers last a long time. Easy to grow. Disease resistant. Sometimes a stingy bloomer. Flowers have a tendency to ball up in cool weather.

FIRST LOVE

ARS Rating: 7.1

Hybrid Tea
Introduced: 1951

Flower: The catalog *Roses* by Fred Edmunds says, "Long, slender, pearly pink buds are both distinctive and exquisite." Blooms are rose-pink with hints of light pink. Double, 2-1/2 to 3-1/2 inches with 25 to 30 petals. Flowers appear singly on long stems.

Fragrance: Moderate.

Form and Foliage: Tall, stately and slender. Graceful, slightly long, light green leaves that perfectly match the character of the buds.

Comments: A free-blooming cross of 'Charlotte Armstrong' and 'Show Girl'. Good cut flower. Performs best in warm areas.

FIRST PRIZE

ARS Rating: 9.0   Introduced: 1970   AARS 1970

Hybrid Tea

Flower: Pink buds up to 4 inches long give way to huge blooms—pink outside and ivory inside. Double, up to 6 inches with 30 to 35 thick, irregular petals. Borne one to a long stem.

Fragrance: Light to moderate. Old-time rose fragrance.

Form and Foliage: Low and bushy. A bit more spreading than most hybrid teas so bushes are normally pruned to inside-facing buds. Vigorous grower. Medium to dark green, leathery leaves cover the entire length of the stem.

Comments: Produces ample quantities of large flowers. Repeats quickly. Exceptionally hardy. Armstrong Nursery considers it "the ultimate in form and beauty." Excellent cut flower. Top exhibition rose. One of only 10 roses with an ARS rating of 9.0 or higher. Somewhat prone to mildew, but easily controlled.

FORTY-NINER

ARS Rating: 7.2   Introduced: 1949   AARS 1949

Hybrid Tea

Flower: A nostalgic bicolor. Cherry red inside with straw yellow outside. The red turns magenta as it ages. Nicely shaped buds open into large, high-centered, 3-1/2 to 4-inch double flowers with 30 to 40 petals.

Fragrance: Slight.

Form and Foliage: Medium height, upright and bushy. Vigorous grower. Glossy, dark green leaves.

Comments: A distinct and novel color combination developed by crossing 'Contrast' with 'Charlotte Armstrong'. Free flowering.

FRAGRANT CLOUD

ARS Rating: 8.0

Hybrid Tea

Introduced: 1968

Flower: Long, scarlet-orange buds slowly open into high-centered, perfectly formed coral blossoms. Double, 4-1/2 to 5 inches with 25 to 30 thick petals. Flowers appear singly and in clusters on long stems.

Fragrance: Strong. Intense, pleasurable, old-time fragrance. As the Armstrong Nursery catalog remarks: "Each flower literally conceals a small perfume factory." James Alexander Gamble Medal for Fragrant Roses, 1969.

Form and Foliage: Upright and husky. Free branching, short to medium in height. Vigorous grower. Lustrous, dark green foliage.

Comments: Easy to grow—excellent for the novice or expert. Disease resistant. Winner of many international awards. Good cut flower.

FRIENDSHIP

ARS Rating: 8.0

Hybrid Tea

Introduced: 1978   AARS 1979

Flower: High-centered, deep pink buds open into large, rich pink blooms with a light touch of salmon-red on the borders of the outer petals. Large, 6-inch double flowers have 25 to 30 petals. Almost perfect example of true hybrid tea form. Long, straight stems.

Fragrance: Strong. Pleasantly sweet.

Form and Foliage: Tall, strong and upright. Vigorous grower. Large, glossy green leaves cover plant.

Comments: A reliable hybrid of 'Fragrant Cloud' and 'Miss All-American Beauty'. Tremendous production of quality blossoms all season. Flowers last a long time on bush or cut. Will not fade or discolor even on hottest days. Hardy and disease resistant.

FUTURA

ARS Rating: 7.5

Hybrid Tea

Introduced: 1975

Flower: Pointed buds open into coral-orange blooms with perfect hybrid tea shape. Double, 4 to 5 inches with 20 to 25 petals. Long stems.

Fragrance: Moderate.

Form and Foliage: Tall, well branched and shapely. Vigorous grower. Covered with dark green leaves.

Comments: Touted as the rose for the gardener who doesn't like to grow roses. Prolific and easy to grow. Color will not fade. Disease resistant. Good cut flower. Hot weather decreases petal count.

GARDEN PARTY

ARS Rating: 8.6

Hybrid Tea

Introduced: 1959   AARS 1960

Flower: Long, urn-shaped, ivory buds with a dab of pink on petal margins open into huge, full, creamy ivory blossoms. Double, high-centered, 4 to 5 inches with 25 to 30 petals. Long, strong stems.

Fragrance: Slight.

Form and Foliage: Upright, bushy and well branched. Medium height. Vigorous grower. Deep olive green, semiglossy foliage.

Comments: An excellent rose which inherited its outstanding characteristics from its famous parents, 'Charlotte Armstrong' and 'Peace'. Flowers are well proportioned with great substance on the bush or cut. A good bloomer. Large amounts of luxuriant foliage. Top exhibition rose. Resists most diseases, but will occasionally mildew.

GRANADA

ARS Rating: 8.8

Hybrid Tea

Introduced: 1963   AARS 1964

Flower: Red and yellow bicolor, urn-shaped buds give way to gaily colored, medium size blossoms. Double, 4 to 5 inches with 20 to 25 petals. Borne singly and in clusters on strong, medium-long stems.

Fragrance: Strong, spicy. Winner of James Alexander Gamble Medal for Fragrant Roses, 1968.

Form and Foliage: Upright and slightly bushy. Medium height. Vigorous grower. Holly-like, toothed foliage.

Comments: The delightful blend of colors and quickly repeated blooms make this rose a favorite. It is favorably compared with 'Talisman', a 1929 hybrid tea of outstanding quality. Long-lasting flowers and distinctive leaves contribute to its overall excellence.

GYPSY

ARS Rating: 6.7

Hybrid Tea

Introduced: 1972   AARS 1973

Flower: Nearly black, dark red, urn-shaped buds burst into a flaming red-orange blossom. Cuplike, double, 4 to 5-inch flowers with 35 to 40 firm petals and erect stems.

Fragrance: Slight. Light and spicy.

Form and Foliage: Very tall, strong and vigorous. Full, dark, bronze green, glossy foliage.

Comments: Flamboyant display of colors holds even in hot weather. Long-lasting fragrance. Very disease resistant. An excellent landscape hybrid tea because of its tall, full foliage. Good cut flower.

HEIRLOOM

ARS Rating: 6.5

Hybrid Tea

Introduced: 1972

Flower: Deep lilac, pointed buds open into magenta blooms that gradually lighten to pure lilac. Double, high-centered, 4 to 5 inches with 35 petals. Borne singly or in clusters on long stems.

Fragrance: Strong. Intense, raspberry-like perfume.

Form and Foliage: Medium to tall and upright. Dark green leaves.

Comments: Generous flower producer. Very vigorous, dark lavender flowers. Disease resistant, but somewhat irregular flower and foliage quality.

HELEN TRAUBEL
Hybrid Tea

ARS Rating: 7.1   Introduced: 1951   AARS 1952

Flower: Well formed, tapered buds open into warm apricot and sparkling pink blooms. High-centered, double, 5 to 6 inches with 20 to 25 petals.

Fragrance: Moderate. Fruity.

Form and Foliage: Tall, very full and bushy. Vigorous grower. Leathery, olive green foliage.

Comments: Long, tapering buds and nodding stems with old tea style. Practically covered with buds. This unusual color combination was developed by crossing 'Charlotte Armstrong' and 'Glowing Sunset'. Takes well to pruning. Makes a fine hedge or screen. Disease resistant.

HONOR
Hybrid Tea

ARS Rating: 7.6   Introduced: 1980   AARS 1980

Flower: Long, pointed buds open to reveal brilliant, white, satiny flowers. Double, 4 to 5 inches with 18 to 25 petals. Long stems.

Fragrance: Light.

Form and Foliage: Tall, upright and stately. Vigorous grower. Dark olive green, leathery leaves.

Comments: Abundant flower producer over a long season. Along with only two other hybrid teas, 'Tropicana' and 'Medallion', it holds the distinction of having won both the Rose of the Year award and All America Rose Selection. Performs well in all types of weather. Excellent cut flower.

IRISH GOLD
Hybrid Tea

ARS Rating: 7.0

Introduced: 1966 as 'Grandpa Dickson' and registered in the U.S. as 'Irish Gold' two years later.

Flower: Pointed buds of pale yellow open into enormous, starburst-shaped, light gold blooms. Double, up to 7 inches across with 30 to 35 petals. Long stems.

Fragrance: Light.

Form and Foliage: Stiff, upright. Medium height. Graceful. Very glossy, dark green foliage.

Comments: A fine yellow rose with huge, long-lasting blooms. Good in cool climates, although flower color will contain a slight pink blush. Upright growth permits planting in narrow areas. Disease resistant.

IVORY TOWER

Hybrid Tea
ARS Rating: 7.5 · Introduced: 1978

Flower: Exquisite, large, pointed, light pink buds open into high-centered blooms of ivory white with a hint of light pink. Double, 5 to 5-1/2 inches with 30 to 40 petals. Borne singly on sturdy, medium length stems.

Fragrance: Moderate. Spicy and fruity.

Form and Foliage: Medium height, bushy and upright. Abundant, clean-looking, semiglossy green foliage.

Comments: Nearly perfect from bud through flower. Good cut flower.

JOHN F. KENNEDY

Hybrid Tea
ARS Rating: 6.0 · Introduced: 1965

Flower: Long, white buds with a tinge of apple green open into pure white flowers. Double, 5 to 6 inches with 45 to 50 petals. Long stems.

Fragrance: Strong. One of the most fragrant white roses.

Form and Foliage: Tall and upright. Vigorous grower. Leathery leaves.

Comments: Huge, pure white blooms do not fade. Free blooming. Best in warm, dry climates. Generally disease resistant, but some susceptibility to mildew.

KENTUCKY DERBY

Hybrid Tea
ARS Rating: 7.8 · Introduced: 1972

Flower: Beautiful, urn-shaped, deep red buds develop into high-centered blooms of the same color. Double, 6 inches with 35 to 45 petals. Borne singly or in clusters on long, strong stems.

Fragrance: Slight.

Form and Foliage: Tall and bushy with many thick canes. Vigorous grower. Large, glossy green leaves.

Comments: Color won't fade on long-lasting blooms. Requires more fertilizer than most. Dependable bloomer. Does well in heat. Disease resistant and hardy. Outstanding cut flower.

JADIS

ARS Rating: 8.0

Hybrid Tea

Introduced: 1974

Flower: Elegant, urn-shaped buds open into vibrant blooms shaded an unusual pink with a hint of lavender. Double. Borne singly on long, straight stems.

Fragrance: Strong. Old-style rose fragrance. Jadis means "days of old" in French.

Form and Foliage: Tall, upright and bushy. Vigorous grower. Excellent hybrid tea form. Large, light green, leathery leaves.

Comments: A 'Chrysler Imperial' and 'Virgo' hybrid with an unforgettably rich fragrance. Prolific bloomer. Disease resistant. Good cut flower.

KING'S RANSOM

ARS Rating: 7.1

Hybrid Tea

Introduced: 1961   AARS 1962

Flower: Long, tapered buds give way to pure golden blooms. Double, high-centered, 5 to 6 inches with 40 to 45 thickly rolled petals. Borne singly on long stems.

Fragrance: Moderate.

Form and Foliage: Tall, upright, vigorous and strong. Beautiful, dark green leaves completely cover the plant.

Comments: Prolific bloomer. Flowers are rarely influenced by weather, producing reliable long-lasting color. Easy to grow. Hardy. Useful as a narrow hedge or for cut flowers.

KORDES' PERFECTA

ARS Rating: 6.9

Hybrid Tea
Introduced: 1957

Flower: Slow-opening buds give way to magnificent, overlapping petals of cream-tipped crimson and yellow. Double, 4-1/2 to 5 inches with up to 70 petals.

Fragrance: Heavy. Old-fashioned tea rose scent.

Form and Foliage: Tall and upright. Vigorous grower. Glossy, serrated, reddish green foliage.

Comments: An erratic rose primarily valued by rose exhibitors seeking the perfect flower. In cool climates, flowers often have green centers. Needs some shade to grow—burns in direct sun. Tends to develop blackspot disease.

LADY X

ARS Rating: 8.4

Hybrid Tea
Introduced: 1966

Flower: Long, slender, pale lavender-pink buds open into large, high-centered blooms of delicate, soft lavender. Borne singly and doubly on straight, sturdy stems.

Fragrance: Light.

Form and Foliage: Well branched and upright. Big, strong and vigorous. Covered with heavy green foliage that has a reddish tinge when new.

Comments: Long-lasting blooms, lavishly produced. It is said that even those who don't normally care for lavender roses should like these. Very few thorns. Likes some shade or cool weather during the growing season. Good cut or exhibition flower. Somewhat disease resistant, but will mildew.

LEMON SPICE

ARS Rating: 7.0

Hybrid Tea
Introduced: 1966

Flower: Long, pointed buds open quickly into loose, high-centered, pale yellow flowers. Double, 4 to 4-1/2 inches with 25 to 30 petals. Weak stems.

Fragrance: Moderate to strong. Spicy.

Form and Foliage: Tall and willowy. Vigorous grower. Large, glossy green leaves.

Comments: Prolific bloomer and very easy to grow. Light yellow color holds well. Relatively few thorns. Disease resistant.

LUSTIGE

Hybrid Tea
ARS Rating: 8.0 Introduced: 1973

Flower: Large, egg-shaped buds quickly open into coppery red blossoms with yellow reverse. Double. Borne singly on long stems.

Fragrance: Moderate.

Form and Foliage: Medium to tall, upright. Abundant, large, glossy green, leathery foliage.

Comments: A cross between 'Peace' and 'Brandenbury', it is a prolific and continual producer of blossoms. Excellent lasting quality. A good size plant with beautiful form. Relatively few thorns.

MEDALLION

Hybrid Tea
ARS Rating: 7.6 Introduced: 1973 AARS 1973

Flower: Long, shapely, buff apricot buds open slowly into extraordinarily large, pale apricot blooms blended with a touch of pink. Double, 7 to 8 inches with 30 to 35 petals. Usually borne one to a long, sturdy stem.

Fragrance: Moderate. Pleasant, fruity fragrance much like ripe apples.

Form and Foliage: Tall, well branched. Bright green, leathery leaves.

Comments: A prolific and continual bloomer. Will last into fall, long after other hybrid teas have quit blooming. Flower color varies due to climate—pinkish in cool weather, more apricot in warm. Relatively few thorns. Disease resistant and good cold hardiness. Useful as a hedge or screen. Long-lasting cut flower.

MIRANDY

Hybrid Tea
ARS Rating: 6.1 Introduced: 1945 AARS 1945

Flower: Huge buds open into immense, full flowers. Starts out garnet red, getting darker with age. Double, 5 to 6 inches with 40 to 50 petals. Usually borne one to a long stem.

Fragrance: Strong. Highly intense perfume scent.

Form and Foliage: Medium height, very bushy. Luxuriant, dark green leaves.

Comments: A cross between 'Night' and 'Charlotte Armstrong', it is one of the finest dark red roses. Prolific. Performs best in high heat and humidity. Bloom shows purple in cooler weather. Useful as a medium-tall hedge.

MISS ALL-AMERICAN BEAUTY
ARS Rating: 8.3

Hybrid Tea

Introduced: 1967   AARS 1968

Flower: According to Stocking Rose Nursery, "The color is rich, deep and might be called shocking pink, but it is not harsh." High-centered, double, 5 to 6 inches with 50 to 60 petals. Usually borne one to a sturdy stem.

Fragrance: Moderate to strong tea fragrance.

Form and Foliage: Tall and shapely. Large, leathery foliage; darker on top than on bottom.

Comments: A 'Chrysler Imperial' and 'Karl Herbst' hybrid that holds its pure, deep pink color from bud stage until the petals fall. Very prolific. Blooms withstand considerable heat. Disease resistant. Good cut or exhibition flower.

MISTER LINCOLN
ARS Rating: 8.7

Hybrid Tea

Introduced: 1964   AARS 1965

Flower: Lovely long, pointed buds open into large, glowing red blooms. Double, 4-1/2 to 6 inches with 30 to 40 petals. Long stems.

Fragrance: Strong. Heavy, rich aroma.

Form and Foliage: Straight and tall. Well branched. Vigorous and strong. Large, dark green, glossy, leathery foliage.

Comments: A 'Chrysler Imperial' and 'Charles Mallerin' cross that is held in high esteem in all parts of the U.S. An excellent choice for the home garden. Easy to grow. Free bloomer, quick to repeat with long-lasting flowers. Velvety textures. Deep fragrance. Red color holds true in all climates. Excellent cut flower and top exhibition rose.

MISTY
ARS Rating: 6.5

Hybrid Tea

Introduced: 1965

Flower: White, pointed, classically shaped buds open into cup-shaped, creamy white blooms. Double, 4 to 5 inches with 50 to 60 petals. Borne in clusters on long, stiff, nearly thornless stems.

Fragrance: Moderate. Tea rose scent.

Form and Foliage: Tall and bushy. Vigorous grower. Attractive, large, leathery, semiglossy leaves.

Comments: Profuse bloomer, but sometimes erratic. Relatively few thorns.

MOJAVE
ARS Rating: 7.6   Introduced: 1954   AARS 1954

Hybrid Tea

Flower: Perfectly formed, tapered buds of burnt orange open into a captivating combination of yellow, pink, burnt orange and vermilion. Double, 4 to 4-1/2 inches with 30 to 35 petals. Borne singly on long, dark stems.

Fragrance: Moderate.

Form and Foliage: Upright, tall and slender. Vigorous. Dark green, semiglossy leaves.

Comments: A hybrid 'Charlotte Armstrong' and 'Signora' that is named after the warm, rich colors of the western desert sunset. Profuse bloomer. Moderate hardiness and disease resistance. Great for cut flowers.

NEW DAY
ARS Rating: 7.0

Hybrid Tea

Introduced: 1977

Flower: Long, pointed buds open into tightly formed, elegant blooms of clear yellow. High-centered, double, 4 to 5 inches with 25 to 30 broad, stiff petals. Borne singly or in clusters on long, straight stems.

Fragrance: Strong. Spicy.

Form and Foliage: Medium-tall, branching from the base. Vigorous and sturdy. Gray-green foliage.

Comments: Never without blooms; produces continually all season. Does exceptionally well in cool weather, but is susceptible to mildew. Good cut flower.

OKLAHOMA
ARS Rating: 7.1

Hybrid Tea
Introduced: 1964

Flower: Deep red buds open into huge, deep red blooms. Double, 6 inches with 45 to 50 petals. Usually borne one to a long stem.

Fragrance: Strong. Intoxicating musk rose scent.

Form and Foliage: Tall and heavily branched. Beautiful form. Dark green, leathery leaves.

Comments: A 'Chrysler Imperial' and 'Charles Mallerin' hybrid. Its color comes the closest of any rose to being black. Long-lasting blooms, excellent form. Superb fragrance. Good cut flower. Very attractive when arranged with white roses. Needs extra protection in colder areas. Susceptible to mildew.

OLDTIMER
ARS Rating: 7.4

Hybrid Tea
Introduced: 1971

Flower: Pointed, apricot-colored buds slowly open into huge blooms of a most unusual color—bronzy apricot with a coppery cast. High-centered, double, 7 inches with 40 to 50 thick, satiny petals. Very long stems.

Fragrance: Light. Fruity.

Form and Foliage: Tall, upright and strong. Vigorous grower. Leathery, glossy green leaves.

Comments: Free blooming, though not profuse. Flowers are long lasting. Hardy. Flowers criticized by some for being "on the loose side."

OREGOLD
ARS Rating: 7.5

Hybrid Tea
Introduced: 1975   AARS 1975

Flower: Oval, pointed, saffron yellow buds quickly spiral open into full, vibrant yellow blooms. High-centered, double, 5 to 6 inches with 35 to 40 petals. Borne singly on long, sturdy, rather thorny stems.

Fragrance: Light. True tea rose scent.

Form and Foliage: Medium height and bushy. Vigorous grower. Classic hybrid tea form. Dark green, oval-shaped leaves.

Comments: Very prolific. Nonfading flowers hold color through blooming period. Disease resistant. Good cut or exhibition flower.

PARADISE

ARS Rating: 8.5   Hybrid Tea

Introduced: 1978   AARS 1979

Flower: Long, perfectly formed, high-centered buds swirl open to become silvery lavender blooms with ruby-edged petals. According to the Armstrong Nursery catalog, it is "the color of kings and clergy." Double, 5 inches with 25 to 30 petals. Stems are long and straight.

Fragrance: Light.

Form and Foliage: Excellent hybrid tea form. Medium to tall and bushy. Glossy, heavy, thick leaves.

Comments: First lavender rose to win AARS. Striking and different. Abundant bloomer with flowers holding color and form very well. Good repeat bloom. Very disease resistant. Good cut and exhibition flower.

PASCALI

ARS Rating: 8.0   Hybrid Tea

Introduced: 1968   ARS 1969

Flower: Tapered buds give way to glistening, creamy white blooms. Medium size, perfectly formed double flowers are 3 to 4 inches with 30 shiny petals. Generally borne one to a long, sturdy stem.

Fragrance: Light to moderate.

Form and Foliage: Erect, upright bush. Very vigorous grower. Full, dark green, glossy leaves.

Comments: Resulted from a cross of 'Queen Elizabeth' and 'White Butterfly'. Free blooming, repeating at least four times a season. Color not affected by weather. Winner of many European awards. Very disease resistant. Freedom from mildew makes it an exception among white roses. Excellent cut flower. Top exhibition rose.

PEACE

ARS Rating: 9.0   Hybrid Tea

Introduced: 1945   AARS 1946

Flower: Large, egg-shaped, primrose buds become globular, golden yellow blooms with subtle, translucent pink tips. Fully double, 5 to 6 inches with 40 to 45 petals. Long, sturdy stems.

Fragrance: Slight.

Form and Foliage: Tall and bushy. Very strong grower. Stiff canes. Covered with glossy, deep green leaves.

Comments: The world's best known rose and a parent of many other popular roses. Long-lasting flowers. Does not generally produce an abundance of blooms, but those it does produce are nearly perfect. 'Peace' has won most of the world's top rose awards, including the National Gold Medal Certificate. It is one of only ten roses with the near perfect ARS rating of 9.0. Disease resistant and hardy. Excellent cut flower or exhibition rose. Prune lightly.

PERFUME DELIGHT
Hybrid Tea

ARS Rating: 7.8   Introduced: 1973   AARS 1974

Flower: Delicate, brilliant pink buds open into satiny blooms of rich pink. High-centered, double, 4-1/2 to 5 inches with 25 to 30 petals. Borne singly atop long, firm stems.

Fragrance: Strong. Spicy, old-time rose scent.

Form and Foliage: Medium height, upright and bushy. Large, leathery, dull, olive-green leaves.

Comments: Includes 'Peace' and 'Chrysler Imperial' in its rather complex heritage. Large quantities of big, bright blooms that continue late into the season are common. Beautiful plant form. Disease resistant. Excellent cut flower. The fragrance of a single bloom fills a room for hours. Fine exhibition flower.

PETER FRANKENFIELD
Hybrid Tea

ARS Rating: 7.9   Introduced: 1966

Flower: Long, well-shaped buds open into beautiful rose-pink blooms. Double, 6 to 7 inches with many petals.

Fragrance: Slight.

Form and Foliage: Vigorous and upright. Plants are well covered in deep green leaves.

Comments: Free blooming, although flower size is not consistently large. Hardy and disease resistant. Good cut flower.

PICCADILLY
Hybrid Tea

ARS Rating: 6.4   Introduced: 1960

Flower: Brilliant scarlet and gold bicolor. Double, 4-1/2 to 5 inches with 25 to 30 petals.

Fragrance: Slight.

Form and Foliage: Medium height, upright and slightly spreading. Vigorous grower. Abundant, large, glossy, dark green leaves.

Comments: Very free blooming. As weather warms, flower color becomes more intense. Useful as a hedge. Tender in extreme cold. Has been frequently used as a parent for many of the popular bicolors. Color fades rapidly.

PINK PEACE

ARS Rating: 7.7

Hybrid Tea

Introduced: 1959

Flower: Quick-opening buds give way to very large, well formed, deep pink blooms. Shapely, double, 5 to 6 inches with 50 to 60 petals. Strong stems.

Fragrance: Strong. Old-fashioned tea fragrance.

Form and Foliage: Tall, upright, sturdy and vigorous. Healthy, heavy green leaves.

Comments: The name is confusing because it is a seedling of 'Peace' rather than a sport. A good rose in its own right with an abundant bloom during the season. Repeats very quickly. Long-lasting blooms on the bush or cut. Somewhat prone to rust and mildew.

PORTRAIT

ARS Rating: 7.5

Introduced: 1971   AARS 1972

Hybrid Tea

Flower: Rich, pink, urn-shaped buds give way to deep pink blooms touched with gold. Double, 3-1/2 to 4 inches with 40 to 45 petals.

Fragrance: Moderate. Old-time rose scent.

Form and Foliage: Fairly tall and strongly branched. Nicely shaped. Dark green leaves cover plant from top to bottom.

Comments: The first AARS winner to be hybridized by an amateur. Parents are 'Pink Parfait' and 'Pink Peace'. Easy to grow—great for the beginner. Free blooming and long lasting. Very hardy and disease resistant.

PRISTINE

ARS Rating: 8.0

Hybrid Tea

Introduced: 1978

Flower: Long, elegant, ivory buds with a touch of pink quickly give way to large, almost white blooms with soft pink edges. Beautifully formed, double, 5 to 6 inches with 25 to 30 petals. Borne singly on long cutting stems.

Fragrance: Slight.

Form and Foliage: Symmetrical. Upright and slightly spreading. Large, reddish green foliage.

Comments: Each flower has a stunning, porcelain appearance. Profuse bloomer. Disease resistant. Excellent cut flower and top exhibition rose.

PROUD LAND
ARS Rating: 7.7   Hybrid Tea   Introduced: 1969

Flower: Long, velvety red buds open into high-centered, bright red blooms. Perfectly formed, double, 4-1/2 to 5-1/2 inches with up to 60 petals. Generally borne one to a long stem.

Fragrance: Moderate. Rich tea rose scent.

Form and Foliage: Tall, very vigorous and upright. Almost as wide as it is tall. Strong and sturdy. Abundant dark green leaves.

Comments: Resulted from a cross of 'Chrysler Imperial' and an unnamed seedling. An extremely profuse bloomer for the entire season. Holds color well, except in extreme heat. Disease resistant but will mildew. Can be used as a hedge or beside tall fences.

RED DEVIL
ARS Rating: 7.6   Hybrid Tea   Introduced: 1970

Flower: Rounded buds slowly open into spectacular, large, bright red blooms with silvery undersides. Double, high-centered, 3-1/2 to 4 inches with up to 60 petals. Long, straight stems.

Fragrance: Slight.

Form and Foliage: Medium height and upright. Vigorous grower. Glossy, dark green leaves.

Comments: Holds color well. Center of the bloom holds its form. Best in cooler climates, although too much moisture in the air causes it to ball. Burns in hot weather. Good for cut flowers and exhibition.

RED MASTERPIECE
ARS Rating: 7.3   Hybrid Tea   Introduced: 1974

Flower: Classic, dark red buds open into huge, rich, red blooms. Beautiful red rose form. Double, 6 inches with 35 to 40 petals. Long strong stems.

Fragrance: Strong. Wonderful old-fashioned rose scent.

Form and Foliage: Good tea form—strong, vigorous and upright. Strong, sturdy canes. Leathery, dark green leaves.

Comments: Profuse bloomer whose form and fragrance can be traced to its 'Chrysler Imperial' heritage. Holds its dark red color well. Does best in warm climates. Excellent cut and exhibition flower. Prone to mildew.

ROYAL HIGHNESS
ARS Rating: 8.4 Hybrid Tea
Introduced: 1962 AARS 1963

Flower: Long, pointed, blush pink buds slowly open into light pink blooms. Double, 5 to 5-1/2 inches with 40 to 50 petals. Generally borne one to a long, sturdy stem.

Fragrance: Strong. Tea rose scent.

Form and Foliage: Tall, upright and medium bushy. Vigorous and strong. Rich, dark green, leathery foliage.

Comments: A 'Virgo' and 'Peace' hybrid that produces lavish amounts of perfectly formed, classic tea-shaped blooms. Superior fragrance. Excellent cut flower. Top exhibition rose. Somewhat more tender to cold than most hybrid teas.

SEASHELL
ARS Rating: 7.5 Hybrid Tea
Introduced: 1976 AARS 1976

Flower: Large, light orange, classic tea-shaped buds open into high-centered, peach-pink blossoms with a soft yellow base. Double, 3 to 5 inches with 35 to 40 long-lasting petals. First appears singly, then in clusters.

Fragrance: Slight.

Form and Foliage: Medium height and upright. Canes are somewhat compact. Symmetrical and vigorous. Thick, holly-like, dark green leaves.

Comments: Abundance of beautiful blooms. Color constantly changes with the weather and with age. Lush foliage. Mildew resistant.

SNOWFIRE
ARS Rating: 5.7 Hybrid Tea
Introduced: 1970

Flower: Red, egg-shaped buds unfold into striking bicolor blooms—deep scarlet inside, pure white outside. Large, flat blooms fall apart fast. Opaque petals have a velvety texture. Double, 4 to 6 inches with 35 to 40 petals.

Fragrance: Light.

Form and Foliage: Low growing and vigorous. Not much spreading. Covered with glossy, dark green leaves.

Comments: Unique and rather spectacular color combination. Plant form and foliage make it a useful and versatile rose for the landscape. Flowers good for cutting. Best in warm climates. Generally disease resistant, but susceptible to mildew.

SPELLBINDER

ARS Rating: 7.0   Hybrid Tea
      Introduced: 1975

Flower: Large, ivory white buds open into high-centered, ivory blooms tinged pink. Blooms darken as the flower ages. Double, 5-1/2 to 6 inches with 25 to 30 petals. Usually borne singly on long, heavy stems.

Fragrance: Slight.

Form and Foliage: Tall and upright with many branches. Very vigorous grower. Abundant, thick, dark green, leathery leaves.

Comments: Profuse bloomer with excellent lasting quality. Disease resistant. Good cut flower. Slow to repeat when young, but improves with age.

STERLING SILVER

ARS Rating: 4.9   Hybrid Tea
      Introduced: 1957

Flower: Pinkish lavender buds gracefully open into glistening silver blooms. Double, flat, 3 to 3-1/2 inches with about 30 firm petals. Produces in clusters similar to a floribunda. Long stems.

Fragrance: Strong. Sweet.

Form and Foliage: Medium height and upright. Glossy green, leathery leaves.

Comments: One of the first true lavender hybrid teas, it resulted from a cross of 'Peace' and an unnamed seedling. Distinctive color, it is popular and widely distributed in the U.S. Does best when pruned lightly and given afternoon shade in warmer areas. Although a shy bloomer and generally lacking vigor, it is a rather stunning cut flower.

SUMMER SUNSHINE

ARS Rating: 7.2   Hybrid Tea
      Introduced: 1962

Flower: Well formed, classic tea buds open into bright, golden yellow blooms. Often described as the yellowest of yellow roses. Double, 5 inches with 20 to 25 petals. Generally borne one to a long stem.

Fragrance: Light.

Form and Foliage: Upright, with a slight tendency to spread. Medium height. Vigorous grower. Glossy green foliage with a gray tinge.

Comments: Color is pure yellow and will not fade or change. Prolific bloomer. Somewhat tender to cold, requires extra winter protection.

SUNSET JUBILEE
ARS Rating: 7.2   Hybrid Tea   Introduced: 1973

Flower: Deep rose colored buds open slowly into blooms of light pink with soft gold and white ribs. High-centered, double, 6 inches with 35 to 40 petals. Long cutting stems.

Fragrance: Slight.

Form and Foliage: Medium height with excellent form. Vigorous grower. Shiny, light green foliage. New growth is bronze-red.

Comments: Named in honor of *Sunset* magazine's 75th anniversary. Large, long-lasting blooms. Disease resistant. Good cut flower. Color may change according to temperature.

SUTTER'S GOLD
Hybrid Tea

ARS Rating: 6.9   Introduced: 1950   AARS 1950

Flower: Long, pointed buds are gold with shades of red. They open into large, high-centered blooms of deep gold with salmon-red shadings on the outside. Double, 4 to 5 inches with 30 to 35 petals. Borne singly on long, dark stems.

Fragrance: Exceptionally strong. Delightfully fruity. James Alexander Gamble Medal for Fragrant Roses, 1966.

Form and Foliage: Upright and tall with medium spread. Vigorous grower. Dark green, glossy, leathery foliage.

Comments: 'Charlotte Armstrong' and 'Signora' hybrid. A dependable performer and excellent for repeat blooms. Large, somewhat loose flowers. Holds color better in cooler weather. Very disease resistant. Good cut flower. Dense enough to use as a screen or hedge. Low exhibition rating is because buds open flat, without form.

SWARTHMORE
Hybrid Tea

ARS Rating: 8.4   Introduced: 1963

Flower: Beautiful long buds quickly open into high-centered blossoms of red and rose-pink edged with deeper red. Borne on long, strong stems.

Fragrance: Slight.

Form and Foliage: Medium to tall, upright and bushy. Sturdy and vigorous. Dark green, leathery leaves.

Comments: Endless production of beautiful flowers. Long lasting on the bush or as a cut flower. Top exhibition rose.

SWEET AFTON

ARS Rating: 7.5

Hybrid Tea
Introduced: 1964

Flower: Large, long, pointed, egg-shaped buds quickly open to become nearly white with blushes of pink on the back side. Double, 4-1/2 to 5 inches with 30 to 40 petals. Borne singly on strong, medium-long stems.

Fragrance: Strong.

Form and Foliage: Tall, spreading and bushy. Vigorous grower. Abundant, leathery leaves.

Comments: Very easy to grow with continual, long-lasting blooms. Does well in hot areas. Disease resistant. Can be used as a hedge or for cut flowers.

TALISMAN

ARS Rating: 4.3

Hybrid Tea
Introduced: 1929

Flower: Long, pointed buds open to medium size, multicolored flowers of red, yellow and copper in varying proportion. Double, 3 to 4 inches with 20 to 25 petals.

Fragrance: Moderate to heavy.

Form and Foliage: Upright, tall and bushy. Very vigorous grower. Bright green, leathery foliage.

Comments: One of the all-time, multicolored favorites, although its climbing form has a better 1980 ARS rating, 5.8, and is grown more often. Free flowering. Good cut flower. Slight problem with mildew.

THE DOCTOR

ARS Rating: 5.9

Hybrid Tea
Introduced: 1936

Flower: As described by Interstate Nurseries: "Long, pointed buds open into simply enormous yet graceful blooms of pink with an iridescence and sheen beyond description." Double, about 6 inches with about 25 petals.

Fragrance: Strong.

Form and Foliage: Small but quite bushy. Light green leaves.

Comments: Considered by many to possess the most beautiful color of any rose. Slow growing, but size and fragrance are well worth the wait. Prune lightly for best results. Good cut flower.

TIFFANY
Hybrid Tea

ARS Rating: 8.8   Introduced: 1954   AARS 1955

Flower: Deep pink, long, pointed buds open into large, perfectly formed, silvery pink blooms touched with subtle golden yellow at the base. Double, 4 to 5 inches with 25 to 30 silky petals. Borne singly on long, sturdy stems.

Fragrance: Exceptional—one of the most fragrant modern roses. James Alexander Gamble Medal for Fragrant Roses, 1962.

Form and Foliage: Upright, tall and slender. Very vigorous grower. Good, crisp, dark green foliage.

Comments: 'Charlotte Armstrong' and 'Girona' hybrid. Very free blooming and long lasting—seldom out of bloom. Color improves in warm weather. Disease resistant. Good cut flower.

TROPICANA
Hybrid Tea

ARS Rating: 8.8   Introduced: 1962   AARS 1963

Flower: Brilliant, orange-red, pointed buds open into huge, cup-shaped blossoms of the same color. Double, 4-1/2 to 5 inches with 30 to 35 petals. Borne singly and in clusters on very long, thorny stems.

Fragrance: Strong. Delightful, heavy fruity scent.

Form and Foliage: Tall, heavily branched and spreading. Exceptionally vigorous. Dark, grayish green, glossy, leathery leaves.

Comments: Very easy to grow. Incredible abundance of flowers that hold their color even in the hottest weather. Cut flowers keep their fragrance as long as a week indoors. Good exhibition flower. Winner of the National Gold Medal Certificate—'Climbing Tropicana' (ARS rating of 7.9) appeared as a sport in 1971. Flower and foliage are identical. Has shown a tendency to mildew.

TYPHOO TEA
Hybrid Tea

ARS Rating: 7.0   Introduced: 1974

Flower: Silver-white buds open into blooms with a contrasting coral-orange cast. In cooler climates, the bloom has a slight salmon-red shade. It becomes more orange in warm areas. Double, high-centered, 4-1/2 to 5 inches with 50 to 60 petals.

Fragrance: Strong. Pleasantly powerful lemon scent.

Form and Foliage: Tall and bushy with slender canes. Very vigorous grower. Small, glossy green leaves.

Comments: A neat, clean plant that produces best when given afternoon shade. Blooms fade and die quickly. Susceptible to blackspot.

WHITE MASTERPIECE
ARS Rating: 7.6

Hybrid Tea
Introduced: 1969

Flower: Classical, egg-shaped buds open into high-centered blooms of pure, shining white. Double, up to 6 inches, with as many as 60 petals. Long, thick, sturdy stems.

Fragrance: Light. Sweet.

Form and Foliage: Low growing and spreading. Large, glossy leaves cover entire plant.

Comments: Produces well all season. Widely adapted to varying climates. Bred especially to resist mildew and blackspot. Good cut flower. Top exhibition rose.

WINI EDMUNDS
ARS Rating: 8.1

Hybrid Tea
Introduced: 1973

Flower: Long buds slowly open into high-centered, bicolored blooms of cherry red with cream to yellow reverses. Double, 3-1/2 to 4-1/2 inches with many petals. Borne on long stems.

Fragrance: Moderate.

Form and Foliage: Tall, upright and vigorous. Dark green, leathery leaves have a copper tinge.

Comments: Very profuse. Good cut flower.

YANKEE DOODLE
ARS Rating: 7.5

Hybrid Tea
Introduced: 1975   AARS 1976

Flower: Long, deep golden yellow buds open slowly into small blooms of light salmon inside with buttery yellow outside. Double, 4 inches with 50 stiff, scalloped petals. Flower form is informal. Long stems.

Fragrance: Light tea perfume.

Form and Foliage: Tall, bushy and vigorous. Very strong and sturdy. Glossy, olive-green leaves completely cover the plant.

Comments: An unusual color combination. Does well in cooler climates. Disease resistant. Good rose for the landscape, but not for the exhibitor who desires better form. Very low rated in southern California.

Floribundas

Floribundas are a modern rose in every way. Compared to hybrid teas, floribundas are more hardy, tougher and more free flowering. Although flowers are not quite as large as those of hybrid teas, they have the same color range. Typically, floribundas make well proportioned flower heads, or groups of individual flowers. Many of the new varieties produce only one or two flowers per stem, more like the hybrid tea. Height varies, but most reach 2 to 4 feet.

Floribundas are outstanding landscape plants. Use them to produce a mass of color equal to annual bedding plants. They are also favored as border, barrier and container plants. Locate them along a driveway or pathway, or in front of taller growing roses such as hybrid teas and grandifloras.

The development of the floribunda is fairly recent, but the name itself is old, belonging to an otherwise forgotten rose of the early 1800's. The name was resurrected in 1950 by J.H. Nicolas, former Research Director of Jackson & Perkins Co.

A NEED FOR A NEW ROSE

D.T. Poulsen, a Danish hybridizer working early in this century, sought a more practical rose. He wanted a rose that would survive the very cold winters of northern Europe and also produce an abundance of flowers all season without special treatment. He began by crossing the *polyantha* roses—dwarf forms of the exceedingly tough hedgerow rose, *Rosa multiflora*—with hybrid teas. His reasoning was simple enough: crossing one parent of outstanding hardiness, and one of great beauty should produce a strain with the virtues of both.

Poulsen was successful in creating a new group of roses. At first they were called the *hybrid polyanthus,* but later became known as the *Poulsen roses.* These were the forerunners of floribundas. Very popular as bedding roses in the 1930's, all were pink or red with no fragrance. 'Else Poulsen', introduced in 1924, is still considered one of the outstanding floribundas. But greater changes were still to come.

After World War II, many floribundas of more modern character appeared. 'Fashion' and the very long-blooming 'Vogue' came from Gene Boerner of Jackson & Perkins. Jack Harkness in Great Britain introduced 'Frensham', perhaps the first floribunda with the classical, hybrid tea-like bud.

In 1949 came 'Masquerade', also from Boerner. This rose marked a turning point for the floribundas. It had all the floribunda characteristics: free flowering, long blooming season and hardiness, but with the added bonus of an exceptionally bright flower. The flower is yellow when it opens, becoming pink and finally scarlet. 'Masquerade' became very popular and brought attention to all floribundas. The special name, *floribunda,* became necessary for this rapidly expanding group of roses at this time. 'Masquerade' also proved to be a prodigious parent and its offspring include many of today's popular floribundas.

There are many nominees for the "world's greatest" floribunda. Some are notable for their flower clusters, others for beautiful individual flowers, and still others for the quantity of flowers.

'Europeana' is near the top of most every list of outstanding floribundas. It is perhaps what Poulsen, given time, would have created. An excellent landscape plant, it is compact, low growing and hardy. Large clusters of well formed, crimson flowers are carried in a balanced, exhibition-quality flower spray. The plant is strong and vigorous, and blooming is continual. Members of the American Rose Society have rated 'Europeana' 8.8 on their scale of 10. It received The Hague Gold Medal in 1962, and was introduced into the United States in 1968.

'Gene Boerner', 'Iceberg', 'Ivory Fashion', 'Rose Parade', 'Little Darling' and 'First Edition' are other outstanding floribundas.

Floribundas are great and largely unsung heroes of the low maintenance garden and landscape. If you are hesitant about growing roses, or think you have a brown thumb, start with a floribunda. If your garden could use a colorful, low maintenance perennial, or you need a lot of color in a tough landscape situation, try a floribunda.

Culture—In most ways, floribundas are treated like hybrid teas. You can follow the same rules when growing floribundas, but less rigorously. Their performance will satisfy most tastes if given only water and one or two applications of fertilizer per season. Periodic grooming, including removal of spent flowers and unproductive twigs, keeps them looking best. Prune more lightly than you would a hybrid tea and remove excessive amounts of twiggy growth from the plant center. For exhibition or bouquet purposes, pinch away the center, dominant bud of a cluster so the others will develop more evenly and make a more attractive spray. To make a thick hedge, plant about 15 inches apart. Two staggered rows will make an impenetrable 4- by 4-foot hedge.

Pruning is not absolutely required, and the quantity of bloom, as at left, is typical throughout the season.

ANGEL FACE

ARS Rating: 8.0   Floribunda

Introduced: 1968   AARS 1969

Flower: Artistic, high-centered, urn-shaped buds open quickly into ruffled blooms of pure lavender with ruby red shadings. Perfectly shaped, double, 3-1/2 to 4 inches with 35 to 40 petals. Borne primarily in clusters.

Fragrance: Strong. Rich, old-fashioned scent.

Form and Foliage: Shapely. Upright but compact and bushy. Dark, glossy green, leathery foliage.

Comments: The only lavender floribunda AARS. Good keeping quality. In hot areas flower color is best when grown in afternoon shade. Hardy and disease resistant. Good cut flower. Top exhibition rose.

ANABELL

ARS Rating: 8.0   Floribunda

Introduced: 1972

Flower: Tight, well formed buds open into orange-pink blooms. Double, 4 inches with 30 petals. Borne singly and in clusters.

Fragrance: Moderate.

Form and Foliage: Medium height, upright and compact. Vigorous grower. Foliage is dense, with small, medium green leaves.

Comments: Abundant blossoms over a long season. Good floribunda form. Disease resistant. Excellent cut flower and popular exhibition rose.

APRICOT NECTAR

ARS Rating: 7.7   Floribunda

Introduced: 1965   AARS 1966

Flower: Egg-shaped buds of deep apricot open into pure apricot, hybrid tea-type blossoms. Double, high-centered, 4-1/2 to 5 inches with 35 to 40 petals. Borne in clusters or one to a medium length stem.

Fragrance: Strong. Fruity aroma.

Form and Foliage: Upright and bushy. Excellent form. Vigorous grower. Dark green, glossy leaves.

Comments: The only buff apricot floribunda. Quick repeater. Holds well and resists fading. Does well in hot climates. Disease resistant and hardy. Keeps well as a cut flower.

BAHIA
ARS Rating: 7.1

Floribunda
Introduced: 1974   AARS 1974

Flower: Coral-orange buds give way to large blooms of vivid orange, sometimes tinged pink. Double, 2-1/2 to 4 inches with 20 to 30 petals. Small clusters.

Fragrance: Moderate. Pleasant spicy aroma.

Form and Foliage: Tall, upright and well branched. Vigorous grower. Covered with glossy, dark green leaves.

Comments: Profuse bloomer. Holds color and shape for a long time. Disease resistant. Useful as a hedge or for cut flowers.

BETTY PRIOR
ARS Rating: 8.3

Floribunda
Introduced: 1935

Flower: Dark carmine, egg-shaped buds open into bright pink, dogwood-like blooms. Single, 2 to 3 inches with 5 petals. Borne in clusters.

Fragrance: Moderate.

Form and Foliage: Medium height and bushy. Vigorous grower. Leathery, dark green leaves.

Comments: This old-timer, released over 45 years ago, still ranks as one of the most prolific flower producers among floribundas. Strong grower. Hardy and disease resistant. Perfect as a border or an edging along walks.

BON-BON
ARS Rating: 7.3

Floribunda
Introduced: 1974   AARS 1974

Flower: High-centered, pointed buds of pink and white open into showy pink and white bicolor blooms. Double, 3 to 3-1/2 inches with 20 to 25 petals. Heavy clusters on short stems.

Fragrance: Moderate.

Form and Foliage: Medium height, bushy and spreading. Very ornamental. Glossy, green leaves.

Comments: A prolific and continual bloomer—at times the plant is completely covered with flowers. Easy to grow and disease resistant. Uniform shape in all climates makes it an excellent choice for a low hedge or border. Long-lasting cut flower. Top exhibition rose.

CATHEDRAL
ARS Rating: 7.5

Floribunda

Introduced: 1975   AARS 1976

Flower: Long, pointed, soft apricot buds become wavy blooms of blazing scarlet-tinted salmon. Double, 3 to 3-1/2 inches with 15 to 18 petals. Borne in small clusters on short stems.

Fragrance: Light to moderate. Sweet.

Form and Foliage: Excellent floribunda form—compact, low and very bushy. Covered with glossy, olive-green leaves tinted copper.

Comments: Small, elegant and long-lasting flower clusters. Very disease resistant. Fine cut flower. Top exhibition rose.

CÉCILE BRUNNER
ARS Rating: 7.2

Polyantha

Introduced: 1881

Flower: Small, pointed, beautifully formed buds give way to petite, delicate, open blooms of light pink with a touch of yellow at the base. Double, 1 to 1-1/2 inches. Borne in enormous sprays on thin stems.

Fragrance: Moderate.

Form and Foliage: Slow growing, dwarf and bushy. Dark green, somewhat sparse foliage.

Comments: An old-timer known as the "sweetheart rose." Long popular as the boutonniere rose. Continual bloomer. Attractive cut flower.

CHARISMA
ARS Rating: 8.0

Floribunda

Introduced: 1977   AARS 1978

Flower: Nicely formed, egg-shaped buds open into brightly colored blooms of bright yellow edged orange and red. The red color intensifies as the flower ages. Double, 2-1/2 inches with 35 to 40 petals.

Fragrance: Light.

Form and Foliage: Medium size, spreading and mound shaped. Leathery, glossy, green leaves.

Comments: An excellent landscape floribunda. Neat, attractive growth habit. Abundant and long-lasting flowers, cut or on bush.

CHERISH
Floribunda

ARS Rating: 8.0 Introduced: 1980 AARS 1980

Flower: Egg-shaped, slightly pointed buds become large, high-centered, vivid shell pink blooms. Double, 3 to 4 inches with 25 to 30 petals. Borne in clusters.

Fragrance: Light. Faint cinnamon scent.

Form and Foliage: Medium size, spreading and compact. Vigorous grower. Well covered in glossy, deep green leaves.

Comments: An excellent floribunda with exceptionally large flowers and attractive, symmetrical plant form. Blooms early and prolifically all season. Performs well under all weather extremes. Long-lasting cut flower.

CHINA DOLL
Polyantha

ARS Rating: 7.6 Introduced: 1946

Flower: Small, long, pointed buds open into small, full, cup-shaped blooms of bright pink. Double, 1 to 2 inches with 20 to 25 petals. Borne in large clusters.

Fragrance: Slight.

Form and Foliage: Dwarf, generally about 18 inches high. Carpet-like and bushy. Vigorous grower. Abundant, medium green, leathery foliage.

Comments: Very prolific continual producer of large flower clusters that almost cover the plant. Excellent for containers or as an edging.

CIRCUS
Floribunda

ARS Rating: 7.3 Introduced: 1956 AARS 1956

Flower: Perfectly formed buds are bright yellow and orange. They become buff orange with shades of pink on the outer petals, and gradually change to cherry red when fully open. Double, 2-1/2 to 3 inches with 45 to 60 petals. Borne in clusters.

Fragrance: Moderate. Spicy tea scent.

Form and Foliage: Low, spreading and compact. Attractive, dark green, leathery leaves cover the plant from top to bottom.

Comments: Succession and intensity of this brightly colored rose change according to weather conditions. Widely used in breeding. Prolific grower. Disease resistant. Makes a fine low hedge.

CIRCUS PARADE
ARS Rating: 6.8

Floribunda

Introduced: 1963

Flower: Urn-shaped buds open into large, multicolored blooms. Colors include yellow, salmon, pink, red and all combinations. Double, 3 to 3-1/2 inches with 30 to 40 petals. Borne in clusters.

Fragrance: Moderate.

Form and Foliage: Upright, bushy and well shaped. Large, leathery leaves.

Comments: A sport of 'Circus' aptly named for its parade of color. Hue and intensity change daily with the weather. Extremely profuse bloomer. Disease resistant.

CITY OF BELFAST
ARS Rating: 8.2

Floribunda

Introduced: 1968

Flower: Perfectly formed, orange buds open into cup-shaped blooms of brilliant orange with a scarlet tint. Double, 2-1/2 to 3 inches with many slightly frilled petals. Borne in clusters.

Fragrance: Slight.

Form and Foliage: Medium size and spreading. Attractively clothed in dark green, glossy leaves.

Comments: Very profuse—always in bloom. Quick repeater. Grows well in any weather. Hardy and disease resistant.

DEEP PURPLE
ARS Rating: 7.8

Floribunda

Introduced: 1980

Flower: Egg-shaped, slightly pointed buds give way to deep lavender blossoms. Double, 3 to 4 inches with 30 to 45 petals. Borne singly and in clusters.

Fragrance: Moderate.

Form and Foliage: Large, upright and bushy. Very vigorous. Glossy, dark green leaves.

Comments: Leaves make an attractive backdrop for the abundance of flowers. Disease resistant.

EUROPEANA
ARS Rating: 8.8   Floribunda

Introduced: 1968   AARS 1968

Flower: Red, pointed buds give way to large, glistening, cardinal red blooms. Double, 3 to 3-1/2 inches with 25 to 30 petals. Borne in huge, heavy clusters.

Fragrance: Slight.

Form and Foliage: Low, compact and spreading. Large, lustrous, bronze-green leaves.

Comments: An excellent, low maintenance, landscape rose. Prolific and long-lasting blooms. Color holds well under all weather conditions. Very disease resistant. Keeps for a long time as a cut flower. Top exhibition rose.

EUTIN
ARS Rating: 7.6   Floribunda

Introduced: 1940

Flower: Carmine red buds, which may be pointed or round, open into cup-shaped, glowing, bright red blooms. Double, 2 to 3 inches with 20 to 25 petals. Borne in great profusion—from 50 to 100 flowers on long, strong stems.

Fragrance: Slight.

Form and Foliage: Medium height, vigorous and robust. Leathery, dark green, glossy foliage.

Comments: A great display of color maintained over a long season has made this variety popular for many years. Well known for its large clusters. Disease resistant. Stunning as a border or when massed. Great for bouquets.

EVENING STAR

ARS Rating: 8.5

Floribunda

Introduced: 1974

Flower: Large, pointed buds open into high-centered white blooms with a pale yellow base. Double, 3 to 4 inches with many petals. Borne singly and in clusters on long, strong stems.

Fragrance: Light.

Form and Foliage: Excellent form—medium height, upright and bushy. Grows vigorously. Large, abundant, dark green, leathery leaves.

Comments: A very attractive garden rose—good in form and flower. Profuse and continual bloom. Long-lasting quality on the bush or cut. Good for exhibition. Disease resistant.

EYE PAINT

ARS Rating: 8.0

Floribunda

Introduced: 1975

Flower: Egg-shaped buds open into stunning scarlet flowers with white centers and bright yellow stamens. Single, 2-1/2 inches with 5 or 6 petals.

Fragrance: Slight.

Form and Foliage: Tall, very dense, spreading and bushy. Abundant small, dark glossy green leaves.

Comments: More of a shrub rose than a typical floribunda. Flowers vigorously and continually. Can be used as a hedge.

FASHION

ARS Rating: 7.9

Floribunda

Introduced: 1949   AARS 1950

Flower: Small, egg-shaped buds tipped with red open into lively, luminous, peach-coral blooms. Double, 3 to 3-1/2 inches with 20 to 25 petals. Borne singly and in small clusters.

Fragrance: Moderate.

Form and Foliage: Medium height, bushy and spreading. Vigorous grower. Attractive, abundant, bronze-green, glossy foliage.

Comments: First coral-colored floribunda. Resulted from a cross of 'Pinocchio' and 'Crimson Glory'. Profuse, continual bloomer. Very little fading. National Gold Medal Certificate, 1954.

FIRST EDITION
ARS Rating: 8.5

Floribunda

Introduced: 1976   AARS 1977

Flower: Small, pointed buds burst into large, nicely formed, bright coral blooms with neon shadings of yellow, orange, pink and red. Semidouble, 2-1/2 inches with 17 to 25 petals. Medium-to-long stems carry blooms singly or in clusters.

Fragrance: Slight.

Form and Foliage: Perfectly mounded. Medium height, compact and vigorous. Dense, glossy, leathery, olive green foliage.

Comments: A beautiful bloom on an attractive plant. Continual production of flowers in showy clusters. Colors darken in cooler areas. Excellent landscape rose—as a low hedge, when massed or as a border. Perfect for containers. Great cut flower. Top exhibition rose.

GINGER
ARS Rating: 8.2

Floribunda

Introduced: 1962

Flower: Bright scarlet-orange buds give way to brilliant, hybrid tea-type, orange-vermilion blooms. Double, 2-1/2 to 3 inches with 25 to 30 petals. Borne singly and in irregular clusters on long stems.

Fragrance: Slight.

Form and Foliage: Low, compact and bushy. Vigorous grower. Shiny, dark green foliage.

Comments: Always in bloom. Relatively thornless. Disease resistant and fairly hardy. Excellent cut flower. Good exhibition rose.

GENE BOERNER

Floribunda

ARS Rating: 8.4   Introduced: 1968   AARS 1969

Flower: Beautifully formed, pointed, pink buds open into hybrid tea-type, perfectly shaped, true pink blooms. Double, high-centered, 3 to 3-1/2 inches with 30 to 35 petals. Long, strong stems hold flowers borne singly or in clusters.

Fragrance: Light. Old-fashioned tea-rose fragrance.

Form and Foliage: Taller than most floribundas—up to 5 feet. Symmetrical, strong and very vigorous form. Covered with light green, glossy leaves.

Comments: One of the more free-flowering floribundas. Long-lasting flowers. Unique shape. Disease resistant. Good cut flower. Top exhibition rose.

GINGERSNAP

Floribunda

ARS Rating: 8.0   Introduced: 1978

Flower: Long, almost urn-shaped buds open into highly ruffled, pure, bright orange blooms. Double, 4 to 4-1/2 inches with 30 to 40 petals. Borne singly or in clusters.

Fragrance: Light. Fruity scent.

Form and Foliage: Medium height, bushy and upright. Vigorous grower. Abundant, glossy, deep green foliage.

Comments: Beautiful spring bloom is often slow to repeat. Slightly tender.

ICEBERG

ARS Rating: 8.6

Floribunda
Introduced: 1958

Flower: Small, slender, crystal white buds open into fairly large, silvery white blooms. Double, 3 to 4 inches, with 35 to 40 petals. Nearly always borne in clusters.

Fragrance: Moderate to strong. Sweet.

Form and Foliage: Nicely shaped, medium height and bushy. Vigorous grower. Covered with shiny green leaves.

Comments: Very free-flowering. Almost thornless. Extremely hardy and disease resistant. Good exhibition rose.

IVORY FASHION

ARS Rating: 8.1

Floribunda
Introduced: 1958   AARS 1959

Flower: Long, slender, creamy white buds slowly spiral open into high-centered, nearly hybrid tea size, clear ivory blooms. Semidouble, 4 to 4-1/2 inches with 15 to 20 petals. Borne in small clusters.

Fragrance: Moderate.

Form and Foliage: Medium size, upright and sturdy. Vigorous grower. Covered with leathery, medium green leaves.

Comments: A free-flowering, stunning white rose. Very disease resistant. Long-lasting cut flower. Good low hedge or screen. Top exhibition rose.

KATHERINE LOKER

ARS Rating: 7.3

Floribunda

Introduced: 1978

Flower: Pointed buds open into formal, high-centered, buttery yellow blooms. Double, 4 to 5 inches with 25 to 30 very broad petals. Flowers overlap 1 to 4 to a cluster.

Fragrance: Slight. Spicy aroma.

Form and Foliage: Mounded. Medium height, upright and spreading. Vigorous grower. Abundant, semiglossy foliage.

Comments: Prolific and long-lasting. Large flowers for a floribunda. Attractive plant.

LITTLE DARLING

ARS Rating: 8.8

Floribunda

Introduced: 1956

Flower: Small, egg-shaped buds give way to perfectly formed, wonderful, hybrid tea-like bicolored blooms of yellow and salmon-pink. Double, 2-1/2 inches with 24 to 30 petals. Borne in clusters.

Fragrance: Moderate. Spicy scent.

Form and Foliage: Tall and very vigorous. Many long arching canes are typical. Dark, glossy, leathery leaves.

Comments: Small but gorgeous flowers on a large plant. Abundant blooms. Disease resistant. Long-lasting cut and top exhibition flower.

MARGO KOSTER

ARS Rating: 7.4

Polyantha

Introduced: 1931

Flower: Round buds open into small, globular, salmon-pink blooms. Double, 1 to 2 inches with many petals. Borne in clusters.

Fragrance: Slight.

Form and Foliage: Compact and low. Abundant, glossy green foliage.

Comments: An old-time rose often available from florists as a potted plant. Free blooming and disease resistant. Makes a nice edging or container plant. Tends to become a little twiggy.

MARINA
ARS Rating: 7.6   Floribunda

Introduced: 1980   AARS 1981

Flower: Large, long, pointed buds spiral open into high-centered orange blooms with some red and gold tones. Double, 2-1/2 to 3 inches with 30 to 40 petals. Borne in clusters on long stems.

Fragrance: Light.

Form and Foliage: Medium height, upright and very bushy. Vigorous grower. The plant is well covered by dark green, glossy leaves.

Comments: Larger flowers than many floribundas. A very prolific and attractive garden rose first introduced to Europe in 1974. Well known as a greenhouse rose. Disease resistant. Good cut flower.

MATADOR
ARS Rating: 8.2   Floribunda

Introduced: 1972

Flower: Medium size, egg-shaped buds resembling rich, heavy, silk slowly open into blooms that are orange on top and light yellow underneath. Double, high-centered, 2 to 2-1/2 inches with 25 to 30 petals. Borne in clusters on long, strong stems.

Fragrance: Slight.

Form and Foliage: Medium height and bushy. Vigorous grower. Many large, leathery, dark green leaves.

Comments: Profuse bloom with excellent lasting quality. Holds color and shape well during entire blooming season. Relatively thorny. Disease resistant. Good cut flower. Top exhibition rose.

MERCI
ARS Rating: 8.0   Floribunda

Introduced: 1976

Flower: Oval buds slowly spiral open to become bright red, hybrid tea-type blooms. Double, 2-1/2 to 3 inches with 25 to 35 thick petals. Borne singly and in clusters.

Fragrance: Light.

Form and Foliage: Medium to tall and symmetrical. As broad as it is tall. Vigorous grower. Excellent form. Attractive, thick, dark green leaves.

Comments: Covered with nearly perfect, bright red blooms all season. Holds color a long time. Easy to grow. Reputation for producing more flowers than any other floribunda. Hardy and disease resistant.

ORANGEADE

Floribunda
Introduced: 1959

ARS Rating: 8.0

Flower: Small buds burst open into bright orange blooms. Semi-double, 2-1/2 inches with 7 petals. Borne in well spaced clusters.

Fragrance: Slight.

Form and Foliage: Medium height and bushy. Grows vigorously. Dark green leaves.

Comments: Very free flowering and long lasting. Hardy. Good cutting and exhibition rose.

PICNIC

Floribunda
Introduced: 1976

ARS Rating: 7.0

Flower: Short, pointed buds open into high-centered, hybrid tea-type blooms of coral with a yellow base. Double, 3 to 3-1/2 inches. Borne in clusters.

Fragrance: Slight.

Form and Foliage: Medium height, upright and heavily branched. Vigorous grower. Leathery, glossy green leaves.

Comments: Inconsistent bloomer. Can be used for cut flowers.

REDGOLD
ARS Rating: 7.8

Floribunda

Introduced: 1971   AARS 1971

Flower: Chrome yellow buds with brick red edges open into large, perfectly formed, orange-red blooms edged with magenta. Double, 2 to 3 inches with 25 to 30 large, stiff petals. Borne singly or in large clusters.

Fragrance: Light to moderate. Fruity.

Form and Foliage: Tall and bushy. Vigorous grower. Glossy green foliage.

Comments: Very decorative plant—a bright spot in any garden. Flowers last a long time on the bush or cut. Very disease resistant.

RED PINOCCHIO
ARS Rating: 7.3

Floribunda

Introduced: 1947

Flower: Egg-shaped buds open into cup-shaped carmine red blooms. Double, 3 to 3-1/2 inches with 25 to 30 petals. Borne singly or in large clusters on long, strong stems.

Fragrance: Moderate.

Form and Foliage: Low, upright, branching and bushy. Beautiful, leathery green leaves.

Comments: Profuse and continual bloomer. Color will not fade. Grows somewhat taller in warmer climates, but also does well in cool areas. Disease resistant. Good cut flower.

SARATOGA
ARS Rating: 7.2

Floribunda

Introduced: 1963   AARS 1964

Flower: Slightly creamy buds open into pure white, gardenia-like blooms. Double, 3-1/2 to 4 inches with 30 to 35 petals. Borne singly and in clusters.

Fragrance: Strong. Old rose aroma.

Form and Foliage: Low and well branched. Almost perfect floribunda form. Healthy, glossy green foliage.

Comments: Very prolific and nearly always in bloom. Holds up well in wind and rain. Disease resistant flowers are long lasting on the plant or cut.

ROSE PARADE

ARS Rating: 8.5

Floribunda

Introduced: 1974   AARS 1975

Flower: Nicely shaped, light pink buds slowly open into blooms of an enchanting blend of pink with peach overtones. Double, 2 to 2-1/2 inches with 25 to 30 petals. Borne in small clusters.

Fragrance: Strong. Rich aroma.

Form and Foliage: Medium height, dense and spreading. Vigorous grower. Glistening, dark green foliage.

Comments: A beautiful landscape rose resulting from a cross of 'Sumatra' and 'Queen Elizabeth'. Profuse bloomer. Very hardy and disease resistant.

SEA PEARL

ARS Rating: 8.4

Floribunda

Introduced: 1964

Flower: Elegant, long, pointed buds open into soft peach-pink blooms with cream and yellow reverses. Double, 4-1/2 inches with 24 petals. Borne in large clusters.

Fragrance: Light.

Form and Foliage: Tall, upright and bushy. Vigorous grower. Dark green leaves.

Comments: Free blooming. Intensity of color will vary with weather. Adapts well to coastal conditions. Good cut or exhibition flower.

SARABANDE
Floribunda

ARS Rating: 8.1   Introduced: 1959   AARS 1960

Flower: Medium size buds open into cup-shaped, bright scarlet-orange blooms with bright yellow stamens. Semidouble, 2-1/2 inches with 10 to 15 petals. Borne in large clusters.

Fragrance: Light.

Form and Foliage: Low and spreading. Semiglossy, green foliage.

Comments: A versatile and much admired landscape rose. Large, brightly colored flower clusters cover the entire plant. Nonfading and quick repeating, continuing over a long season. Ideal for border, bedding or foreground. Widely adapted to cultural and climatic extremes, but superb in cool-summer areas. Top exhibition rose.

SIMPLICITY
Floribunda

ARS Rating: 8.0   Introduced: 1979

Flower: Long, pointed buds open into pink blooms. Semidouble, 3 to 4 inches with 18 to 20 petals. Borne in clusters.

Fragrance: Slight.

Form and Foliage: Tall, bushy and upright. Heavily branched and dense—excellent landscape rose. Large, medium green leaves.

Comments: Very free flowering from spring to fall. Very dense growth habit makes it an excellent hedge. Presently available by mail order only.

SPANISH SUN

ARS Rating: 6.3

Floribunda

Introduced: 1966

Flower: Pointed buds give way to large, hybrid tea-shaped blooms of sunny golden yellow. Double, 2-1/2 to 3 inches with 35 to 45 petals. Borne singly or in clusters on long, strong stems.

Fragrance: Strong. Fruity, old rose fragrance.

Form and Foliage: Low, compact and bushy. Vigorous grower. Large, glossy, bright green leaves.

Comments: Very fragrant—one bouquet will perfume an entire room with its scent. Cut flowers last for days. Hardy and disease resistant. Excellent cut flower.

SPARTAN

ARS Rating: 7.1

Floribunda

Introduced: 1955

Flower: Well formed and pointed burnt orange buds open into high-centered, orange-red blossoms. Double, 3 to 3-1/2 inches with 30 petals. Borne singly or in clusters.

Fragrance: Strong.

Form and Foliage: Medium size, upright and bushy. Very vigorous. Dark, glossy green, leathery leaves.

Comments: Prolific bloomer. Flowers a bit larger than most floribundas. Frequently used parent in floribunda breeding program. Disease resistant.

SUNSPRITE

ARS Rating: 8.0

Floribunda

Introduced: 1977

Flower: Egg-shaped buds open into one of the brightest yellow blooms available. Double, cup-shaped blooms open wide enough to show brown stamens. Width 3 inches with 25 to 30 petals. Borne in clusters.

Fragrance: Moderate to strong.

Form and Foliage: Medium size and upright. Vigorous grower. Well clothed in dark green leathery leaves.

Comments: The bright yellow rose against deep green foliage makes an attractive color combination. Free blooming, continuous and unfading. Disease resistant.

THE FAIRY
Polyantha

ARS Rating: 8.4   Introduced: 1941

Flower: Small, coral-pink buds give way to large, arching clusters of button-like, baby pink blooms. Double, 1 to 1-1/2 inches with many petals.

Fragrance: Slight.

Form and Foliage: Medium height, thick and spreading. Sturdy and vigorous grower. Small, shiny, light green leaves.

Comments: An easy to grow, old-time favorite that is still very popular. Profuse bloomer. Small leaves give the plant a fern-like texture. Should be only lightly pruned. Disease, pest and drought resistant—does well in less than ideal conditions. Hardy. Can be used as a ground cover or in borders.

TRUMPETER
Floribunda

ARS Rating: 8.0   Introduced: 1977

Flower: Egg-shaped buds become open, flashy, brilliant, orange-red blooms. Double, 2-1/2 to 3 inches with 35 to 45 wavy petals. Borne in clusters.

Fragrance: Slight.

Form and Foliage: Medium height and bushy. Vigorous grower. Shiny green foliage.

Comments: Prolific and continual bloomer. Disease resistant. Colors are magnificent in mass plantings.

Grandifloras

Grandifloras are the newest of all rose classes. To rose *aficionados,* they are the most problematical. Established in 1954, the grandifloras include some of the most outstanding garden roses, but differences between a grandiflora and a hybrid tea, or a grandiflora and a floribunda are often quite small.

Grandifloras are intermediate between their hybrid tea and floribunda parents—except in height. Most grow taller than either parent. They produce quantities of flowers like a floribunda and the flowers have the size and delicate form of a hybrid tea. The great rose 'Queen Elizabeth' fits this description perfectly, but many varieties are less easily categorized. 'Granada' and 'Duet', both officially classed as hybrid teas, were introduced as grandifloras. 'Apricot Nectar' was introduced as a grandiflora but is now considered a floribunda.

As modern roses are repeatedly interbred, the neat class distinctions will fade. This has happened with the grandifloras and will occur more often with other rose classes as well.

Queen Elizabeth—The grandiflora class was created especially for 'Queen Elizabeth'. The result of a cross between the hybrid tea 'Charlotte Armstrong' and the floribunda 'Floradora', it is one of the outstanding roses of all time.

'Queen Elizabeth' is essentially an oversized hybrid tea that produces wonderful, hybrid tea-like, pink flowers in sprays. It is vigorous and disease resistant.

Even before it was generally available and grown only in test gardens around the country, most observers fell in love with it and hoped it could become an All-America Rose Selection. But there was considerable disagreement as to whether it was a hybrid tea or a floribunda. Its hybridizer, Dr. Lammerts, had originally considered it a floribunda, but then plants grew to the unfloribunda-like height of 8 feet. To eliminate this confusion and so it could become an All-America Rose Selection, the class *grandiflora* was created.

Without 'Queen Elizabeth' there would likely be no grandiflora class today. Its place in the world of roses is well deserved. Its ARS rating is an exceptionally high 9.0. It is a top exhibition rose and rose societies around the world have bestowed upon 'Queen Elizabeth' their most prestigious awards. In fact, the Fourth World Rose Convention held in Pretoria, South Africa in 1979 acclaimed 'Queen Elizabeth' to be "the world's favorite rose." 'Queen Elizabeth' is said to be *the* rose for a one-rose rose garden. 'Queen Elizabeth' is also available in a climbing form, and as a tree rose.

There are many other notable grandifloras. One of them is 'Pink Parfait'. It is a fairly compact-growing grandiflora with more of a hybrid tea character. It is rarely out of bloom and literally covers itself with flowers from spring to frost. 'Pink Parfait' was introduced in 1960 and was chosen to be an All-America Rose Selection in 1961. Its ARS rating is high—8.4.

Uses—Most grandifloras grow, 6 to 8 feet tall. Some, such as 'Prominent', 'Sonia' and 'Olé', are a more compact 4 to 5 feet. Most have inherited improved disease resistance and cold hardiness from the floribundas or gained beautiful flowers from the hybrid teas. Many are useful in more rigorous landscape situations. Frequently, grandifloras are recommended for use as tall hedge, screen or background plants. Most produce long-stemmed flowers that are excellent for cutting.

Culture—Grandifloras are grown much like hybrid teas. One of the differences that may arise is yearly pruning. Most grandifloras are extra vigorous and should be allowed to grow to their full size. For instance, the average cane height after pruning for 'Queen Elizabeth', should be 3 to 4 feet. The cut ends of thick canes should be protected with a wound sealer to prevent dieback or borer damage.

In 1979, 'Queen Elizabeth', left, joined 'Peace' in the rose "Hall of Fame." Of all roses, excluding 'Peace', it was acclaimed the world's favorite.

'Love' grandiflora

AQUARIUS

Grandiflora

ARS Rating: 7.3   Introduced: 1971   AARS 1971

Flower: Long, tight, deep pink buds quickly open into light pink flowers with deep pink margins. Double, 3-1/2 to 4-1/2 inches with 30 to 40 petals. Generally borne singly on long stems, but also borne in clusters.

Fragrance: Moderate.

Form and Foliage: Tall and slender, but not as tall as most grandifloras. Large, heavy, reddish green leaves.

Comments: Produces very freely and holds well even in hot weather. Sturdy and strong. Superior disease resistance and hardiness. Very long lasting as a cut flower. Top exhibition rose.

ARIZONA

Grandiflora

ARS Rating: 6.5   Introduced: 1975   AARS 1975

Flower: Long, urn-shaped buds open into shapely, high-centered blooms of golden orange, bronze and pink. Double, 4 to 4-1/2 inches with 35 to 40 petals. Long, straight, thorny stems hold flowers borne singly or in clusters.

Fragrance: Strong. Delightfully intense.

Form and Foliage: Tall and slender. Leathery, semiglossy, bronze-green leaves.

Comments: Handsome, unique orange coloring. Will not fade. Disease resistant. Can be used as a narrow hedge. Excellent for cut flowers.

BUCCANEER

Grandiflora

ARS Rating: 6.8   Introduced: 1952

Flower: Large, urn-shaped buds open into cup-shaped blooms of beautiful buttercup yellow. Double, 3-1/2 to 4 inches with 25 to 30 petals. Borne singly or in clusters of 2 or 3 on a long stem.

Fragrance: Moderate. Tea scent.

Form and Foliage: Very tall and upright. Vigorous grower. Glossy, dark green, leathery leaves.

Comments: Free blooming. Will not fade in heat. Needs a lot of space. Can be used as a tall hedge. Good cut flower.

CAMELOT
ARS Rating: 7.7   Introduced: 1964   AARS 1965   Grandiflora

Flower: Large, rounded buds open into pale salmon, cup-shaped blooms, perhaps the largest of all grandiflora flowers. Double, 4-1/2 to 5 inches with 50 to 55 petals. Generally borne in clusters on long, straight stems.

Fragrance: Light to moderate. Spicy.

Form and Foliage: Tall and spreading. Vigorous grower. Clothed in large, heavy, holly-like, glossy green leaves.

Comments: This cross between 'Circus' and 'Queen Elizabeth' requires quite a bit of growing space. Flower color changes with the weather, from an orange similar to 'Tropicana' to orange-pink. Clean foliage makes it an attractive background or hedge. Good cut flower. Top exhibition rose.

CARROUSEL
ARS Rating: 7.6   Grandiflora
Introduced: 1950

Flower: Rich red buds open into large, dark red, velvety blooms shaped like hybrid tea blossoms. Semidouble, 3 to 4 inches with 15 to 20 petals. Generally borne in small clusters, but also borne singly.

Fragrance: Light to moderate.

Form and Foliage: Very tall, symmetrical, bushy and upright. Vigorous with strong canes. Leaves are glossy dark green and leathery.

Comments: Profuse producer of long-lasting flowers. Color holds well—practically unfading. Clean looking, disease-resistant foliage. National Gold Medal Certificate, 1954. Can be used as a hedge.

COMANCHE
ARS Rating: 7.5   Introduced: 1968   AARS 1969   Grandiflora

Flower: Bright scarlet, urn-shaped buds give way to large, nicely shaped, brilliant scarlet blooms. Double, 3-1/2 to 4-1/2 inches with 45 to 50 petals. Borne singly or in small clusters on long stems.

Fragrance: Slight.

Form and Foliage: Tall and bushy. Vigorous grower. Large, bright green, leathery leaves have just a hint of red.

Comments: A very colorful rose which produces an abundance of flowers and repeats quickly. Disease resistant. Good cut and exhibition flower.

JOHN S. ARMSTRONG
Grandiflora
ARS Rating: 7.3   Introduced: 1961   AARS 1962

Flower: Beautiful, egg-shaped buds open quickly into high-centered, glowing, deep red blooms, brushed with jet black at the tips. Double, 3-1/2 to 4 inches with 35 to 45 velvety petals. Borne singly and in clusters.

Fragrance: Light.

Form and Foliage: Tall, bushy and strong. Vigorous grower. Deep green, leathery, semiglossy leaves.

Comments: A cross between an unnamed seedling and 'Charlotte Armstrong', named in honor of the founder of Armstrong Nurseries. Known primarily for its beauty in bud stage. Still, it is easy to grow and a continuous bloomer. Disease resistant. Flower tips tend to burn in hot sun.

LOVE
Grandiflora
ARS Rating: 7.3   Introduced: 1980   AARS 1980

Flower: Short, pointed buds give way to brilliant, bicolored blooms with petals of scarlet red inside, silvery white outside. Double, 3-1/2 inches with 35 recurved petals form a star-shaped flower. Generally borne singly.

Fragrance: Light. Spicy.

Form and Foliage: Upright and symmetrical but a rather small grandiflora. Plants are fully covered in rich green leaves.

Comments: Very free blooming over a long season. Good cut and exhibition flower.

MONTEZUMA
Grandiflora
ARS Rating: 7.7   Introduced: 1955

Flower: Beautifully formed, long, slender buds of vivid orange-scarlet open into lighter salmon-orange blooms in warm weather, and into coral-salmon blooms in cool weather. Double, high-centered, 3-1/2 to 4 inches with 30 to 40 petals. Generally borne one to a long stem.

Fragrance: Light to moderate.

Form and Foliage: Tall, bushy and free branching. Vigorous grower. Semiglossy, leathery leaves.

Comments: A prolific bloomer that produces many long, slender buds. Easy to grow. Does well in cool climates. Disease resistant. Beautiful cut flower. Top exhibition rose. National Gold Medal Certificate, 1961.

MOUNT SHASTA
ARS Rating: 7.7

Grandiflora

Introduced: 1963

Flower: Long, slender, crystal white buds slowly open into large, pure white flowers. Double, 4-1/2 to 5 inches with 20 to 30 petals. Generally borne one to a long stem.

Fragrance: Moderate.

Form and Foliage: Upright and tall. Very vigorous grower. Soft, gray-green, leathery foliage.

Comments: A grandiflora in height and vigor, but resembles a hybrid tea in all other respects. Resulted from a cross between 'Queen Elizabeth' and 'Blanche Mallerin'. Does exceptionally well in cool climates. Good disease resistance for a white rose. Needs upward space—good against a post or pillar. Good cut flower. Top exhibition rose.

OLÉ
ARS Rating: 7.7

Grandiflora

Introduced: 1964

Flower: Large, well formed blooms of vermilion red. Has unusual frilled and ruffled petals that make it look like a carnation. Different from any other rose. Double, 3-1/2 to 4 inches with 40 to 45 waxy petals.

Fragrance: Moderate.

Form and Foliage: Somewhat shorter and more spreading than most grandifloras. Very bushy. Shiny, dark green, holly-like foliage.

Comments: Very profuse and long-lasting blooms. Spectacular in full bloom. Attractive foliage. Disease resistant. Excellent cut flower. Top exhibition rose.

PINK PARFAIT
ARS Rating: 8.4

Grandiflora

Introduced: 1960   AARS 1961

Flower: Petite, stylish, urn-shaped buds open into high-centered, well-formed blooms of exquisite color—a pink and cream blend. Double, 3-1/2 to 4 inches with 20 to 25 petals. Big head of bloom. Generally borne one to a narrow stem.

Fragrance: Slight.

Form and Foliage: Medium height, upright and bushy. Heavily branched and vigorous. Abundant, leathery, semiglossy, green leaves.

Comments: Very prolific. Strong growth. Disease resistant. Good cut flower. Top exhibition rose. Has a tendency to fade in hot weather.

PROMINENT
ARS Rating: 7.8   Grandiflora   Introduced: 1971   AARS 1977

Flower: Small, egg-shaped buds open into medium size, star-shaped blooms of brilliant hot orange. Double, high-centered and small compared to most grandiflora, 2-1/2 to 3-1/2 inches with 25 to 30 stiff, recurved petals. Usually borne singly, occasionally in clusters.

Fragrance: Light. Fruity.

Form and Foliage: Medium to tall and bushy. Stately and upright. Dull green foliage.

Comments: Continuous show of long-lasting moderate size blooms. Resembles a greenhouse rose. Disease resistant. Color will not fade on the bush or as a long-lasting cut flower. Top exhibition rose.

QUEEN ELIZABETH
ARS Rating: 9.0   Grandiflora   Introduced: 1954   AARS 1955

Flower: Pointed buds of luminous salmon-pink give way to clear, fresh pink globular-shaped blooms with ruffled petals. Double, 3-1/2 to 4 inches with 35 to 40 large petals. Borne singly and in clusters on long, graceful stems.

Fragrance: Moderate.

Form and Foliage: Very tall and bushy. Very vigorous grower. Beautiful, heavy, glossy deep green leaves. Stems almost thornless.

Comments: An excellent garden rose. First of the grandifloras and the highest rated. Produces an endless supply of long-lasting blooms. Extremely vigorous and very hardy. One of only ten 9.0 or higher rated roses. Known for its disease resistance. Can be used as a hedge, screen or background. Great cut flower, exhibition rose. National Gold Medal Certificate, 1960.

SCARLET KNIGHT
ARS Rating: 7.8   Grandiflora   Introduced: 1966   AARS 1968

Flower: Blackish red buds open into satiny, deep red blooms. Double, high-centered, 4 to 5 inches with 30 to 35 petals. Generally borne 2 to 3 flowers to a cluster.

Fragrance: Slight.

Form and Foliage: Medium height, upright and bushy. Leathery, medium green leaves.

Comments: Color holds well and will not blue. Profuse bloomer. Thornier than average. Disease resistant. Long lasting as a cut flower. Good exhibition rose.

SONIA
ARS Rating: 8.0

Grandiflora

Introduced: 1974

Flower: Satiny, classic-shaped buds open into high-centered, luminous, camellia-like, coral-pink blooms. Color is richest in cool weather. Double, 3-1/2 to 4 inches with 25 to 30 petals. Generally borne one to a stem.

Fragrance: Strong. Sweet and fruity.

Form and Foliage: Tall and well branched, though somewhat smaller than most grandifloras. Glossy, dark green leaves.

Comments: A very popular florist's rose in the United States and Europe. Tremendous production of long-lasting flowers. Disease resistant. Excellent cut flower. Top exhibition rose.

SUNDOWNER
ARS Rating: 7.5

Grandiflora

Introduced: 1978   AARS 1979

Flower: Well formed, egg-shaped buds of gleaming orange slowly open into large, golden orange blooms with tints of salmon. Double, high-centered, 3-1/2 to 4 inches with 35 to 40 petals. Usually borne singly on very long stems. Blooms sometimes clustered late in the season.

Fragrance: Strong. Spicy.

Form and Foliage: Tall, upright and bushy. Vigorous grower. Large, glossy, dark green leaves have copper tints.

Comments: Aptly named, its color is as brilliant as a summer sunset. Profuse. Disease resistant.

WHITE LIGHTNIN'
ARS Rating: 7.4

Grandiflora

Introduced: 1980   AARS 1981

Flower: Long, pointed buds open into dazzling white flowers sometimes edged light pink. Double, 3-1/2 to 4 inches with 24 to 35 gently scalloped petals. Borne in clusters.

Fragrance: Strong. Wonderful citrus scent.

Form and Foliage: Short for a grandiflora but with a very attractive, upright bushy habit. Glossy, deep green leaves.

Comments: A compact, ornamental plant with a prolific bloom and delightfully fragrant flowers. Good cut flower.

Climbers

There are as many different kinds of climbing roses as other rose types. An old, simple definition is, "Climbers are the most vigorous forms of the various groups of roses." Climbers, then, are basically oversized versions of other kinds of roses.

Climbing roses come in all the colors of modern roses. They can grow to 10 to 50 feet. They don't actually climb like ivy or grapes, attaching themselves as they grow. Climbing roses must be tied or otherwise attached to a supporting structure such as a wall, post, pergola or trellis and trained to grow in the desired direction. Without support most climbers will sprawl on the ground or form a mound of tangled growth. In a large garden, such nontraining may produce a charming effect. Modern gardeners typically have smaller gardens and tend to favor the more moderate-growing and easily trained climbing roses.

Generally, the most vigorous-growing climbing roses have the shortest, but most dramatic blooming period. Moderate-sized climbers typically produce flowers throughout the season.

LARGE-FLOWERED CLIMBERS

Of the many kinds of climbing roses, those classified as large-flowered climbers are most important. The name distinguishes them from old-fashioned, small-flowered ramblers. Their stout, stiff canes range in length between 8 and 15 feet. Their flowers vary in diameter between 2 and 6 inches and usually occur in open clusters of up to 25 individual flowers. Most have a distinct, peak bloom time, then varying degrees of repeat bloom. Large-flowered climbers are fairly resistant to pests and cold temperatures. If winter low temperatures reach zero degrees (−18° C) in your area, a simple mound of soil 1 to 2 feet high over the crown of the plant will provide adequate protection. If the canes do winterkill, dieback will stop at the soil mound.

Pillar roses—Most pillar roses are a less vigorous growing form of a large-flowered climber. A pillar is any kind of post, so a pillar rose is simply a rose trained to an upright post. Many climbers can be trained in this fashion, but some are better suited to the technique than others. A good pillar rose grows to about 10 feet high and flowers from top to bottom, not just at the top. With the energy spared from cane production, pillar roses normally produce more flowers than their long-caned cousins. Training a rose to a narrow, upright pillar is a very dramatic way to display a climber and requires relatively little garden space.

Pruning—One advisor recommends leaving as many canes as possible and only removing those that "threaten the peace of the garden." But some varieties are so rampant they will quickly overtake a garden and require judicious cutting back. Flowers develop on short, 6 to 12-inch laterals that arise from 2 and 3-year old canes. In spring just before buds break, shorten these laterals to 3 to 6 inches (or 3 or 4 buds). In summer, remove faded flowers to prevent seed production and promote repeat bloom of repeat flowering varieties. Occasionally remove the oldest, dark brown canes so that new ones may take their place.

CLIMBING SPORTS

The other important kind of climbing rose is the climbing *sport*. Botanists apply the word sport to any naturally occurring mutation. Normal bushes occasionally put out a cane of particularly vigorous growth without growth-stopping flower buds at its tip. Foliage buds taken from such canes retain this characteristic and most all of the other characteristics of the bush variety. When these buds are grafted to their own rootstock, they become a climbing rose. 'Climbing Charlotte Armstrong' is a climbing sport of a hybrid tea. There are a few climbing sports of floribundas. 'Climbing Queen Elizabeth' is a climbing grandiflora. These climbers are easily recognized by their names—the word climbing (or sometimes the abbreviation "Cl.") always precedes the regular name.

Climbing sports flower best if trained horizontally, such as along a fence. The flow of hormones within the canes is altered and more lateral, flower-bearing shoots develop.

'Royal Sunset', left, a large-flowered climber, produces flowers throughout the season on long and strong stems. Repeat bloom is excellent, but is further encouraged if flowers are removed as soon as they begin to fade and droop.

An arbor of climbing roses surrounds a garden of floribundas at Old Westbury Gardens, Long Island, New York.

Built in 1903, the arbor is constructed of black locust. It was first planted with ramblers 'Pink Dawn' and 'Dorothy Perkins'.

Newer varieties such as 'Golden Showers' and 'Climbing First Prize' cover the arbor now.

Varieties are selected by Mrs. Ettieanne Boegner, daughter of the family that created Old Westbury Estate.

Walkway leading to the Old Westbury rose garden is bordered by flowers and climbing roses trained to a chain link fence.

In midwinter you can clearly see how pruned climbers are trained against the fence.

A tunnel of roses at Planting Fields Arboretum, Oyster Bay, Long Island, New York.

The tunnel at left in January. The simple but effective training is clearly visible.

Climbing sports produce more flowers if their canes are arched or trained somewhat horizontally to a wall, fence or trellis. Bending the canes will cause new, flower-bearing growth along the arched stem. Climbing sports will not bloom well if trained to the more upright, pillar position.

Climbing sports are least hardy of the popular climbers. They are safe only where temperatures stay above 20°F (−7°C) through winter. Laying canes on the ground and covering them with soil will protect them to temperatures in the −10°F (−23°C) range.

The great virtue of climbing sports is their beautiful flowers. They have the same large, well formed bud and flower of the parent bush. In some cases, flower quality is even slightly improved by the sport variety. However, many climbing sports do not give as good repeat bloom as their bush varieties. 'Climbing First Prize' is slow to repeat bloom. A faithful repeat bloomer, magnificent in the autumn, is 'Climbing Mrs. Sam McGredy'.

Pruning—Allow climbing sports to establish during the first few years and grow to the height you desire. Then bend the canes, tying them to a fence or trellis. The flowering shoots will grow from these bent canes. For many years the same canes will produce flowering shoots. Each time you prune, shorten the flowering shoots or laterals to 3 to 6 inches. Prompt removal of faded flowers will hasten repeat bloom. For largest possible flowers, remove all the lateral growth of the previous year. A series of long stems will arise from the horizontally strung canes, each bearing a magnificent bloom.

OTHER CLIMBING ROSES

Ramblers are an older type of climbing rose. They have a casual, romantic appeal and are still available from specialist nurseries. Established as a class around 1900, they are derived from the almost prostrate *Rosa wichuraiana* or *R. multiflora*. These roses have long, soft, pendulous canes which require a support of some kind. Canes average 15 to 20 feet long but may grow longer. 'Dorothy Perkins' is a famous rambler that was introduced in 1901. 'Evangeline' is a Walsh rambler introduced in 1906. Its fragrant, single flowers appear in huge dogwood-like trusses. 'Chevy Chase' is one of the last ramblers, which many consider the best. Introduced in 1939, flowers are small and red. The leaves are mildew resistant.

In most situations, ramblers need a lot of pruning. Without an annual overhaul, they accumulate a considerable quantity of unsightly dead wood. All types flower on one-year old canes, so every year it is best to remove all canes that are two years old or older. In informal garden situations this annual pruning is probably less important.

The rambler 'Evangeline' was planted 10 years ago at the base of this ash tree by its present admirer, Bob Cowden. It has never been pruned so there's lots of dead wood inside, but each spring flowers are as profuse as this. Ramblers are excellent for covering old buildings, or as you can see, trees.

Ramblers are extremely hardy and can survive most winters unprotected. If temperatures are sure to drop below −10°F (−23°C), protect plants by placing a loose mulch over the plant's crown. Flowers appear once per season and are limited to red, pink, yellow and white colors. Many varieties are seriously susceptible to mildew.

Trailers and creepers are terms used to describe rambling roses that distinctly prefer to grow horizontally over the ground. Many make excellent ground covers. See page 56.

Kordesii climbers are a new class of climbing roses, introduced by the German hybridizer Wilhelm Kordes in the 1950s. These are moderately sized, low-maintenance roses. They are available in a range of colors and are the most hardy of all climbing roses—most will survive temperatures to −30°F (−34°C) with no special protection.

'Blaze'

'Blaze'

ALTISSIMO

ARS Rating: 8.8

Large-flowered climber
Introduced: 1967

Flower: Large buds unfold into deep scarlet, almost blood red blooms, shaded crimson. Anthers are bright golden brown. Single, 4 inches with 7 petals. Borne in small clusters.

Fragrance: Slight.

Form and Foliage: Tall growing. Abundant, dark green leaves.

Comments: This is an imported climber, very popular in Europe, that has now established a considerable following in U.S. rose societies. Bloom is intermittent but outstanding.

AMERICA

ARS Rating: 8.0

Large-flowered climber
Introduced: 1976   AARS 1976

Flower: Pointed, coral buds open into large, full, salmon-pink, outstanding, hybrid tea-type blooms. Double, 4 to 5 inches with 30 to 35 petals generally appearing in clusters on new wood.

Fragrance: Strong. Delightful carnation-like scent.

Form and Foliage: Medium vigor. Sturdy canes eventually cover a large area. Small, clean, leathery, grayish green leaves.

Comments: Easy to grow. Has been called the perfect climber. Profuse bloomer throughout season. Spectacular color. In some areas, flower form gets top rating. Rivals that of the best hybrid teas. Disease resistant and hardy. One of only four AARS climbers since 1940. Can be used as a pillar rose.

BLAZE (Improved Paul's Scarlet)

ARS Rating: 7.7

Large-flowered climber
Introduced: 1932

Flower: Scarlet buds give way to cup-shaped, blazing red blooms. Double, 2 to 3 inches with 20 to 25 petals. Borne in large clusters.

Fragrance: Slight.

Form and Foliage: Medium to large, vigorous grower to 10 or 15 feet. Dense, dark green, leathery leaves.

Comments: One of the most widely planted roses in the United States. Showy, hardy, easy to grow and fast growing. Thrives everywhere. Covered with blooms all season. Holds color even in hot areas. 'Blaze' is a cross between 'Paul's Scarlet Climber' and 'Gruss an Teplitz', so it is sometimes called "improved" or "everblooming" 'Paul's Scarlet'. Disease resistant.

BLOSSOMTIME

ARS Rating: 7.6

Large-flowered climber
Introduced: 1951

Flower: Beautiful, egg-shaped buds give way to large, high-centered blooms of cameo pink. Double, 3 to 3-1/2 inches with 40 to 50 petals. Borne 2 or 3 to a cluster.

Fragrance: Strong. Tea scent.

Form and Foliage: Small to medium height. Generally upright and more controllable than most climbers, growing to only 6 or 7 feet. Abundant, glossy, bronze-green foliage.

Comments: Profuse and continual bloomer. Color won't fade. Perfect for small fence, pillar or corner area.

CLIMBING CÉCILE BRUNNER   Climbing polyantha
ARS Rating: 7.8   Introduced: 1894

Flower: Small, long, pointed, pink buds open into dainty pink buds with a yellow base. Double, 1-1/2 to 2 inches with many petals. Borne in open clusters.

Fragrance: Moderate. Tea scent.

Form and Foliage: Rather sparse dark green foliage. Vigorous grower to 20 feet or more.

Comments: Climbing version of the "Sweetheart rose" (polyantha 'Cecile Brunner'). Blooms freely in heavy clusters. Blooms mainly in spring, but has many tiny, pink flowers the entire summer. Can be used as a hedge. Strong grower; will spill over fence or balcony.

CLIMBING CHARLOTTE ARMSTRONG   Cl. hybrid tea
ARS Rating: 7.4   Introduced: 1950

Flower: Long, pointed, blood red buds open into large, deep pink blooms. Double, 3 to 4 inches with 30 to 35 petals. Borne in clusters on long stems.

Fragrance: Strong.

Form and Foliage: Upright and very vigorous. Dark green, leathery leaves.

Comments: Abundant bloomer that repeats well. Strong grower with masses of flowers. Train on a large arbor, trellis or fence.

CLIMBING CHRYSLER IMPERIAL   Climbing hybrid tea
ARS Rating: 7.8   Introduced: 1957

Flower: Large, long, pointed buds open into classic-shaped, high-centered, dark red blooms. Double, 4-1/2 to 5 inches with 40 to 50 petals.

Fragrance: Strong. Rich, spicy scent.

Form and Foliage: Long, heavy canes. Very vigorous grower. Abundant, semiglossy leaves.

Comments: Individual blooms last a long time but are a bit slow to repeat. Best in hot summer climates. Susceptible to mildew.

CLIMBING CRIMSON GLORY   Climbing hybrid tea
ARS Rating: 7.1   Introduced: 1946

Flower: Large, long, pointed buds open into cup-shaped, dark, velvet crimson blooms. Double, 4 to 5 inches with 25 to 30 petals.

Fragrance: Strong. Intense damask aroma.

Form and Foliage: Medium size (8 to 12 feet), upright and bushy. Vigorous grower. Abundant, leathery, green leaves.

Comments: An excellent climbing rose considered by some to be better than the bush 'Crimson Glory'. Profuse, long-lasting flowers. A bit slow to repeat—first bloom is best. Prefers warm areas. Very hardy. Can be trained as a bush.

'Climbing Cécile Brunner'

'Climbing Charlotte Armstrong'

'Climbing Dainty Bess'

'Climbing Mrs. Sam McGredy'

'Climbing Etoile de Hollande'

CLIMBING DAINTY BESS

Climbing hybrid tea

ARS Rating: 7.9   Introduced: 1935

Flower: Long, pointed buds open into light pink flowers with distinctive, dark red stamens. Single, 3-1/2 to 4 inches with 5 petals.

Fragrance: Moderate.

Form and Foliage: Large shrub with medium vigor, reaching 8 to 10 feet high. Leaves are leathery and dark green.

Comments: Free blooming over a long period. Disease resistant. Use as shrub or pillar rose.

CLIMBING ETOILE de HOLLANDE

Cl. hybrid tea

ARS Rating: 7.6   Introduced: 1931

Flower: Large, bright crimson, open blooms. Double, cup-shaped to 6 inches are produced on long stems.

Fragrance: Strong. Damask scent.

Form and Foliage: Moderate growth rate to about 8 feet with an open habit. Leaves are soft green.

Comments: Noted rosarian Roy Hennessey wrote, "Really a breathtaking climber on a south wall where it can take more heat than most reds. Blooms early with huge, fragrant, crimson blooms." Color does not fade in heat. Excellent for cutting.

CLIMBING FIRST PRIZE

Climbing hybrid tea

ARS Rating: 8.0   Introduced: 1976

Flower: Large, long, pointed, pink, urn-shaped buds open into very large, high-centered blooms of deep pink with light silver reverses. Double, up to 6 inches, with 30 to 35 petals borne on long stems.

Fragrance: Moderate.

Form and Foliage: Medium height and spreading. Vigorous grower. Dark green, leathery foliage.

Comments: Free blooming in spring, fewer blooms the rest of the year. Huge blooms are sometimes larger than bush variety. Fast growing and hardy. Good cut flower. Top exhibition rose. Use as hedge or on a trellis or fence.

CLIMBING MRS. SAM McGREDY

Climbing hybrid tea

ARS Rating: 6.7   Introduced: 1940

Flower: Tapered buds become very full salmon blooms. Double, 4 to 5 inches wide with 30 to 40 petals. Borne on long stems.

Fragrance: Moderate to strong.

Form and Foliage: Vigorous grower. New growth is red-bronze, slowly becoming glossy green.

Comments: Very free flowering. Stocking Rose Nursery says, "We unhesitatingly recommend this as one of the very finest climbers." Easy care except for end-of-season pruning. Well adapted as fence or wall rose.

CLIMBING PEACE

Climbing hybrid tea

ARS Rating: 7.1   Introduced: 1950

Flower: Classic, golden yellow buds with touch of pink at tips give way to large blooms of golden yellow edged with pink. Double, 4 to 5-1/2 inches with 40 to 50 ruffled petals. Borne on long, strong stems.

Fragrance: Slight.

Form and Foliage: Tall and vigorous. Long, heavy canes. Dark green, leathery leaves.

Comments: Very fast growing, climbing version of the popular hybrid tea. Flowers best when trained horizontally. Doesn't bloom well until established. Use as a hedge, on a fence, arbor or pergola. Splendid cut flowers.

CLIMBING SNOWBIRD

Climbing hybrid tea

ARS Rating: 6.7   Introduced: 1949

Flower: Long, pointed buds become double, high-centered, white-tinged, yellow blooms with creamy white centers. Full and flat when completely open.

Fragrance: Strong.

Form and Foliage: Vigorous but compact grower. Leaves are soft green and leathery.

Comments: White climbing roses are not common and this is perhaps one of the best. Best in southern areas where winters are relatively warm.

'Climbing Snowbird'

CLIMBING SUTTER'S GOLD

Climbing hybrid tea

ARS Rating: 7.3   Introduced: 1950

Flower: Large, long, pointed buds give way to high-centered, deep gold blooms shaded orange and red. Double, 4 to 5 inches with 30 to 35 petals. Borne in clusters.

Fragrance: Strong. Identical to the shrub form 'Sutter's Gold'. Scent has been compared to honeyed fruit.

Form and Foliage: Tall, upright and very vigorous. Dark green, leathery leaves.

Comments: Intermittent bloomer. Not very hardy to cold. Good for narrow places. Can be grown on trellis or as pillar rose.

DON JUAN

Large-flowered climber

ARS Rating: 8.6   Introduced: 1958

Flower: Deep red, pointed buds quickly open into large, velvety red blooms. Double, 4 to 5 inches with 30 to 35 petals. Borne singly or in clusters on long stems.

Fragrance: Strong.

Form and Foliage: Best suited as pillar rose. Medium height, narrow and vigorous. Dark green, leathery leaves.

Comments: Profuse bloomer all season with long-lasting flowers. Needs winter protection. Disease resistant. Excellent hybrid tea-type blossoms are great for cutting. Perfect for narrow areas.

'Don Juan'

'Dortmund'

'Golden Showers'

'Handel'

DORTMUND

Kordesii climber

ARS Rating: 8.6 Introduced: 1955

Flower: Long, pointed buds become 3-inch, bright red blooms with white centers. Single, 5 to 7 petals. Up to 20 blooms develop in large clusters several times per season.

Fragrance: Light.

Form and Foliage: Very vigorous climber that grows to about 8 feet high. Leaves are glossy light green.

Comments: Use as a climber, a free-growing, tall, mounding shrub or peg down as a ground cover. Accepts some shade. Very disease resistant and winter hardy.

DR. J.H. NICOLAS

Large-flowered climber

ARS Rating: 6.5 Introduced: 1940

Flower: Pink, egg-shaped buds open into large, round, rose-pink blooms. Double, 4-1/2 to 5 inches with 45 to 50 petals. Borne in clusters of 3 to 4 to a long stem.

Fragrance: Heavy.

Form and Foliage: Medium height, upright and slender. Dark green, leathery leaves.

Comments: Profuse bloomer with flowers similar to the old style hybrid perpetuals. Disease resistant. Perfect for narrow areas. Can be used as pillar rose.

GOLDEN SHOWERS

Large-flowered climber

ARS Rating: 7.2 Introduced: 1956 AARS 1957

Flower: Bright yellow buds fade into high-centered, well-shaped, daffodil yellow, flat blooms. Double, 4-1/2 to 5-1/2 inches with 25 to 30 petals. Borne singly in great profusion or in clusters on long, strong, almost thornless stems.

Fragrance: Slight.

Form and Foliage: Medium height, 8 to 10 feet, and self supporting with long, strong stems. Glossy, dark green, leathery leaves.

Comments: Profuse and everblooming from top of plant to bottom. Very strong canes. Disease resistant and hardy. Train on fence or trellis, or as a natural pillar.

HANDEL

Large-flowered climber

ARS Rating: 8.6 Introduced: 1965

Flower: Light pink buds open into ruffled, pale pink blooms edged deep pink. Double, 3-1/2 to 4 inches with 20 to 25 petals. Generally borne singly but also in clusters of 2 or 3.

Fragrance: Slight.

Form and Foliage: Medium height. Glossy, brownish green leaves.

Comments: This everblooming variety blooms strongly the first year after planting. Prolific bloomer from top of plant to bottom. Easily trained for small areas. Use as fence climber or pillar.

HIGH NOON

ARS Rating: 6.7

Climbing hybrid tea

Introduced: 1946   AARS 1948

Flower: Bright, golden yellow buds with a touch of red open into pure yellow blooms that lighten after opening. Double, 3 to 4 inches with 25 to 30 petals. Generally borne singly on long, strong stems.

Fragrance: Light. Spicy.

Form and Foliage: Medium height, upright and vigorous. Rich green, leathery foliage.

Comments: Continuous bloomer. Flowers open quickly into mass of yellow. Disease resistant. Good cut flower. Use as climber or pillar.

JOSEPH'S COAT

ARS Rating: 7.1

Large-flowered climber

Introduced: 1964

Flower: Cardinal red buds turn orange before opening into kaleidoscopic blooms ranging from bright yellow to cardinal red. Double, 3 to 4 inches with many petals. Borne in clusters.

Fragrance: Slight.

Form and Foliage: Small to medium size and vigorous. Glossy, grayish green foliage.

Comments: Prolific bloomer all season long. Full range of bright colors on the plant at one time, often in the same cluster. Versatile plant can be used as free-standing shrub, pillar or climber. Somewhat tender to cold and susceptible to mildew. Relatively thorny.

'Joseph's Coat'

NEW DAWN

ARS Rating: 7.9

Large-flowered climber

Introduced: 1930

Flower: Pink flowers turn white in summer. Double, 2 to 3 inches with many petals. Borne in small clusters on long stems.

Fragrance: Slight.

Form and Foliage: Tall, upright and spreading. Extremely vigorous grower. Glossy, dark green foliage.

Comments: A sport of 'Dr. W. Van Fleet', and the first rose to be patented. Produces continually throughout the season. Very hardy. Can be used to cover banks, as pillar or for cut flowers.

PAUL'S SCARLET CLIMBER

ARS Rating: 7.0

Large-flowered climber

Introduced: 1916

Flower: Red buds open into blazing scarlet blooms. Semidouble, 2 to 3 inches with 15 to 20 petals. Borne in large clusters.

Fragrance: Slight.

Form and Foliage: Medium height and vigorous. Leathery, dark green leaves.

Comments: One of the most popular red climbers for years. Produces profuse mass of scarlet blooms once per year in the spring. Blooms will not fade. Flexible stems train easily. Useful as hedge, pillar rose or on fence. Extremely cold hardy.

'Paul's Scarlet Climber'

'Piñata'

'Piñata'

PIÑATA
ARS Rating: 7.0

Large-flowered climber
Introduced: 1978

Flower: Short, egg-shaped buds of light yellow and red open into high-centered blooms of yellow edged in vermilion. Double, 2-1/2 to 3 inches with 25 to 30 petals. Borne in clusters of up to 15 blossoms.

Fragrance: Slight.

Form and Foliage: Well behaved climber. Small to medium height. Not too vigorous. Lushly covered with oval, semiglossy, green leaves.

Comments: One of the most colorful climbers. Very heavy bloomer. Easy to train, not often unruly. Perfect for the small garden or fence. Adaptable as a pillar rose.

RED FOUNTAIN
ARS Rating: 7.0

Large-flowered climber
Introduced: 1975

Flower: Deep red buds are nearly black, then open into dark red flowers, described by Stocking Rose Nursery as "blackish velvet." Double, 3-inch flowers. Large clusters produced in great abundance.

Fragrance: Strong.

Form and Foliage: Vigorous grower. It climbs 10 to 12 feet high. Dark green leaves are somewhat leathery.

Comments: A good floribunda-type pillar rose. After it reaches its ultimate height, the plant cascades back to the ground. Profuse bloom. Very disease resistant.

RHONDA
ARS Rating: 7.9

Large-flowered climber
Introduced: 1968

Flower: Round, salmon-pink buds open into pink blooms with coral overtones. Double, 3 to 3-1/2 inches with 60 petals. Usually borne in small clusters.

Fragrance: Light. Old-fashioned rose aroma.

Form and Foliage: Small—easily handled. Good pillar rose. Glossy, deep green foliage.

Comments: One of the earliest bloomers in spring. Covered with flowers from top to bottom. Disease resistant. Unaffected by heat and rain. Easily trained into pillar or restrained climber.

ROYAL FLUSH
ARS Rating: 8.3

Large-flowered climber
Introduced: 1970

Flower: Egg-shaped, yellow buds open into cream colored blooms with pink edges. Cream color gradually turns white. The whole bloom becomes a light purple before petals fall. Semidouble, 3 to 4 inches, and borne in small clusters.

Fragrance: Moderate.

Form and Foliage: Vigorous, upright, climbing to about 6 feet high. Abundant, dark green, leathery leaves.

Comments: Prolific bloom continues through summer. Long-lasting flowers on bush or cut. Relatively thornless. Hardy.

ROYAL GOLD

ARS Rating: 7.4

Large-flowered climber
Introduced: 1957

Flower: Hybrid tea-type, yellow buds give way to golden yellow flowers. Double, 3 to 4 inches with 30 to 40 petals. Borne singly and in clusters on long, strong stems.

Fragrance: Light. Fruity.

Form and Foliage: As a pillar rose, grows vigorously to 6 or 8 feet. Glossy, green leaves.

Comments: Does not produce mass of color, but flowers do not fade. Easy to prune and train. Relatively thornless. Can be used as pillar or climber. Good cut flower.

ROYAL SUNSET

ARS Rating: 8.1

Large-flowered climber
Introduced: 1960

Flower: Orange, hybrid tea-type, egg-shaped buds open into very large, apricot blooms. Double, 4-1/2 to 5 inches and about 20 petals. Heat reduces color to creamy white. Flowers are cup-shaped on long, strong stems.

Fragrance: Moderate to strong. Fruity scent.

Form and Foliage: Grows vigorously to about 6 feet high. Leaves are thick, glossy green.

Comments: Blooms profusely all season. Disease resistant.

'Royal Sunset'

TEMPO

ARS Rating: 7.5

Large-flowered climber
Introduced: 1975

Flower: Deep red buds open into brilliant red blooms. Double, 3-1/2 to 4 inches with many petals. Borne in many clusters.

Fragrance: Slight.

Form and Foliage: Moderate grower, easily trained horizontally or vertically. Vigorous grower. Dark green, glossy, leathery leaves.

Comments: Excellent quality. One of the earliest to bloom in spring. Deeper color than large-flowered climber 'Blaze' with more and larger blooms. Produces an abundance of long-lasting flowers. Easy to train on trellis, arbor or fence or for use as pillar.

WHITE DAWN

ARS Rating: 7.3

Large-flowered climber
Introduced: 1949

Flower; Medium size buds open into high-centered, gardenia-like, snow white blossoms. Double, 2 to 3 inches with 30 to 35 petals. Borne in clusters.

Fragrance: Moderate.

Form and Foliage: Medium size and very vigorous. Abundant, glossy green foliage.

Comments: The first hardy, everblooming climber. Continual bloomer. Disease resistant.

'Tempo'

Miniatures

Miniature roses are natural dwarfs with perfectly scaled-down flowers and leaves. They have all the beauty, form and color of full-size roses, and they have a character and charm all their own.

Most miniature roses have compact, wiry stems with diminutive leaves and closely spaced flowers. Some have solitary flowers, while others bear flowers in clusters. Flowers are red, pink, white, yellow, orange, peach, lavender, mauve, or blends and multicolored.

There are many advantages to growing minis. They are generally inexpensive, they fit into much smaller spaces compared to full-size roses and they are just as easy to grow.

Many kinds—The average miniature rose grows to about 1 foot high if planted in open soil, a little shorter in a container. Most are characterized by a resemblance to a particular kind of full-size rose. Floribunda miniatures make bushy plants with everblooming clusters of flowers. Hybrid tea miniatures have larger, high-centered flowers and longer, slow-opening buds. Moss minis are duplicates of centifolia moss roses, complete with moss-like hair covering their stems and buds.

The other categories of miniature roses relate to size. "Micro" minis are the smallest. They make 6 to 8-inch plants with flowers as tiny as 1/4 inch in diameter. These are preferred for indoor and container culture. "Macro" minis are at the other end of the scale. These may grow as large as 3 feet high and have flowers 2 inches in diameter.

There are also climbing miniatures, some of which produce 5 to 7-foot canes, and miniature tree roses that stand 1-1/2 feet tall.

A very practical group of miniature roses is in be-

Miniature roses shown at left are unsurpassed as border plants. They are low, colorful and perennial.

tween climbers and bush types in habit. They will grow a foot or so high and spread a few feet in all directions. These are finding favor as ground covers and hanging basket plants.

Origins—Ancient Chinese art includes illustrations of dwarf roses, so some believe miniature roses originated in China. But as Ralph Moore, miniature rose hybridizer, wrote, "I believe that *Rosa rouletii* (or *R. chinensis minima,* the original miniature rose) may not be as old as supposed. It may even be a fairly recent seedling from one of the old China cultivars such as 'Old Blush.' "

History does tell us that European traders first brought miniature roses from Asia to Europe in the 1700's. The plants had some following in England and France in the early 1800's, where they were commonly known as "fairy" roses. They gradually became less popular, until the early 1900's.

In 1918, miniature roses were rediscovered. The history of modern miniature roses starts with a few plants found growing in a Swiss village. These plants were named *Rosa rouletii,* and became very popular. Unlike previous generations, this was the time of scientific hybridizing. *R. rouletii* was soon crossbred with standard and species roses that brought new colors, forms and fragrances to the tiny plants.

Tom Thumb—The popularity of *R. rouletii* encouraged two rose hybridizers in particular. A Dutch hybridizer, Jan de Vink, crossed it with the bright orange polyantha, 'Gloria Mundi'. As a result, 'Tom Thumb' was introduced into the United States in 1936.

'Tom Thumb' was the first mini rose to become popular in the U.S. Since that time, hundreds more have been introduced. In fact, the center of mini rose hybridizing has now shifted from Europe to America.

Jan de Vink went on to develop many of the original mini roses of high quality. By crossing 'Tom Thumb' with 'Ellen Poulsen', a polyantha, the miniatures 'Red Imp' and 'Pixie' were created. A cross of 'Tom Thumb' and the old, popular 'Cécile Brunner' resulted in the miniature 'Cinderella'.

The other hybridizer, a German named Mathias Tantau, crossed 'Tom Thumb' with the floribunda 'Masquerade' to make the still-popular 'Baby Masquerade'.

Miniature rose hybridizing is now dominated by a few Americans. Ralph Moore of Sequoia Nurseries has developed several good miniature roses. He introduced *Rosa wichuraiana* with its spreading growth habit into his breeding line to produce the many spreading, ground cover mini roses for which he is noted. For many years he has worked with the miniature moss roses. He has many brilliantly colored mini rose flowers to his credit.

Other breeders in the United States have made lasting contributions. Lyndon Lyon of New York has worked to increase the hardiness of the mini roses. To that end, he has bred into his minis the rugged species *Rosa rugosa* and *R. acicularis*. Harm Saville of Nor' East Mini Roses in Massachusetts has been particularly successful in developing rich, deep colors. Ernest Williams of Mini Roses in Texas is noted for his ability to add the form and beauty of a hybrid tea to a miniature rose.

More than 400 varieties of mini roses have been introduced since the time of 'Tom Thumb'. Future mini roses will feature stronger, more fade-resistant flower colors, and the distinct fragrances of old-fashioned roses. In the near future, the niche of the miniature rose, both as a perennial bedding plant and a speciality indoor plant, will be firmly established.

Culture—Miniature roses require the same amount of light as larger roses. Some shade is desirable, but about six hours of direct morning or afternoon sun is best. Cultural requirements parallel full-size roses. Soil should be enriched and well drained, the water supply should be generous and fertilizer applied regularly. The one important difference is that the shallow roots of mini roses are more subject to environmental extremes. A mulch applied to the root zone will help improve the root environment. Water may be needed more frequently. High nitrogen fertilizer that might burn should be applied with care.

It is very important to note the maximum size a given variety will become in your geographic area. They are usually 10 to 18 inches high in open soil—but others grow to 3 feet and some to no more than 6 inches. Do not expect a mixed selection of mini roses to grow to the same size.

In areas of moderate winters, plants will grow larger than in cold winter regions. Containers will restrict growth as will poor soil. For these reasons, the specific heights listed in some catalogs are not as helpful as the descriptions "extra vigorous, tall grower," or "macro" mini.

If you need a row to be even in height, consider planting one variety. The problem is, you won't really know if you are successful until you have let the row grow for 2 seasons.

Miniature roses are just as heat tolerant and a little more cold tolerant than hybrid teas. They are safe with no protection to 15° F (−9° C). Below that, simply cover them during winter with loose, noncompacting mulch, such as pine needles.

Miniature roses are not sold bare root. Local nurseries will have them available year-round, usually in 4-inch plastic pots. Larger kinds may be potted into 1-gallon containers. Mail order nurseries (page 53) will ship mini roses with rootballs intact in a moisture-retaining wrapping.

Plant mini roses at or slightly below their nursery level. This differs from the advice given for larger roses. The reason is that mini roses grow on their own roots. They have not been grafted or budded to another variety rose more suitable as rootstock. Planting deeper promotes more root development along the upper section of the stem. Space plants about a foot apart to make a dense planting or thick row.

Pruning needs vary with the plant. Some of the micro minis need no pruning, while some macro kinds are best served by somewhat severe pruning in spring, and some touch-up trimming throughout the season. Let the plant be your guide.

As with large roses, cut at an angle just above an outward-facing bud. Open the center of the plant by reducing the number of twigs. Covering pruning wounds with a sealer is not usually important because the wounds are so small. Use your own judgment—if the cut stem is particularly thick, sealing may help.

Container culture—Any container that provides at least 6 inches of soil depth and has drainage holes is okay for mini roses. The best container size will vary with plant size. Water and fertilizer should be applied more frequently than with plants in the ground.

It is most important for roses in containers to have a soil mix that drains fast yet has good retention of water. The soil must also permit good air circulation. Many commercially available potting mixes, such as Jiffy Mix, Jiffy Mix Plus, Super Soil, Metro Mix, Redi-Earth and others, meet these standards. A 2 cubic-foot bag of a commercial mix is enough soil for 35 to 40 6-inch pots.

To make 2 cubic feet of your own mix, use:
  1 cubic foot sphagnum peat moss
  1 cubic foot propagation-grade perlite
  10 tablespoons ground limestone
  5 tablespoons single superphosphate 0-20-0
  2 tablespoons potassium nitrate 13-0-44
  1 teaspoon iron chelate

Propagation—Mini roses are easier to propagate than full-size roses. Of the two methods used, the most common is by cuttings. A cutting is a section of a stem that is planted, forms roots and becomes a whole plant. Simply select about 3 inches of medium to young growth in the spring or fall and cut if off just below a 5-leaflet leaf. The bud will be the base of the cutting. Stick the cutting into a pot or flat of straight perlite, vermiculite or potting soil. Keep the cutting in a humid environment by covering with a jar or plastic tent. Or, keep them in a corner that receives only morning sun. Check periodically for root formation.

A less common method of propagation is by division. Most mini roses can be divided every three years. Division is beneficial for miniatures that become excessively woody above the ground. It is a technique developed in south Texas and first reported by Dr. Lionel V. Patenaude of San Antonio. Dr. Patenaude outlines the steps to take when propagating by division: "1) First dig all the new holes and prepare soil mix prior to the time of actual division. 2) Cut away about half of the top growth of plants to be divided. 3) Dig the bush out and wash all soil from the roots with a hose. Prune away any broken or diseased roots and trim the ends of all the other roots to stimulate feeder root growth. 4) Judge where to cut through the plant crown. To do so, examine the root structure from all angles. Look at the top growth for perspective, imagining how the bush will look after it is cut. Try to cut so that you have two or more roots on each half. Some plants can be divided three ways, but usually a two-part division works best. You can use a pair of pruning shears to make the cut, but a light pruning saw usually works best. 5) After the cut is made, prune the top growth to one or two inches and place both halves into a pail of water. 6) Plant both halves as if they were two new bushes."

Indoors—Miniature roses require a lot of light to grow and flower. Few homes have sufficient natural light, so you should plan to employ one of these two methods.

The easiest way is to grow roses in pots outdoors until they flower, then bring them inside for display. Healthy plants in a sunny, indoor spot, such as a windowsill, will continue to flower for several weeks. Eventually, flowering will cease and the plants will languish—that's the time to put them back outside.

For miniature roses kept indoors year-round, use supplemental lighting systems. Four or eight-foot fixtures with a combination of cool white and warm white fluorescent tubes work quite well. Some growers prefer the newer tubes designed specifically for plants.

Fluorescent lights should be close to the plants, about 6 to 8 inches from the foliage canopy. They should be on 12 to 16 hours a day. Use an automatic timer to control them. Observe your plants for a time and you can tell the minimum number of hours necessary. Under lights, plants grow constantly and need to be fertilized at a constant rate. A diluted feeding with each watering is best.

Ideal daytime temperatures are between 70° and 80° F (21° and 27° C). A 10° F (6° C) drop at night allows a productive rest. Relative humidity should be 50 to 70 percent. A heated living room in winter may have only five percent relative humidity, so for good growth you will likely have to add moisture to the air. There are several kinds of humidifiers available. A simple evaporative pebble tray under the pots will contribute much moisture to the air around the plant's leaves or you can move your plants to your basement, which is usually more humid.

Micro minis are the best varieties to grow under lights. They are the most compact and easiest to manage. Plus, their minute flowers and leaves are best appreciated up close.

Top: Three hanging baskets of 'Red Cascade'. Bottom, left to right: 'Tu Tu', 'Fashion Flame', 'Over the Rainbow', 'Lavender Jewel', 'Rise 'n Shine', a second 'Rise 'n Shine' and 'Pacesetter'.

'Beauty Secret'

'Cinderella'

BEAUTY SECRET

Miniature

ARS Rating: 9.0   Introduced: 1965

Flower: Long, pointed, bright red, hybrid tea-type buds open into high-centered blooms of medium red. Double, 1 to 1-1/2 inches and borne in clusters.

Fragrance: Strong. Sweet.

Form and Foliage: Medium height, upright and bushy. Vigorous grower. Small, glossy, dark green, leathery leaves.

Comments: Long-time favorite. Prolific and dependable. Does well under lights. Good cut flower. Top exhibition rose. ARS Award of Excellence, 1975.

BO PEEP

Miniature

ARS Rating: 7.6   Introduced: 1950

Flower: Dainty, egg-shaped, soft pink buds open into small, cup-shaped, rose-pink blooms. Double, 3/4 to 1 inch with 20 to 25 petals.

Fragrance: Slight.

Form and Foliage: Very low and bushy. Vigorous grower. Small, glossy green leaves.

Comments: Very prolific bloomer. Attractive habit.

CINDERELLA

Miniature

ARS Rating: 8.9   Introduced: 1953

Flower: Dainty, white, egg-shaped buds open into small, round, satiny white blooms with a touch of pink in center. Double, 1/2 to 1 inch with 40 to 60 petals. Borne in clusters.

Fragrance: Moderate. Spicy.

Form and Foliage: Low to medium height, compact, with arching branches. Covered with small, glossy green leaves.

Comments: One of the finest miniatures. Prolific bloomer with heaviest show in spring. Nearly thornless. Healthy and disease resistant. Can be grown in hanging baskets. Good cut and exhibition flower.

CRICRI

Miniature

ARS Rating: 7.4   Introduced: 1958

Flower: Small, globular buds become salmon-coral blooms. Double, 2 inches, borne singly and in clusters.

Fragrance: Slight.

Form and Foliage: Medium to tall. Loosely compact and bushy. Vigorous. Medium green, leathery leaves.

Comments: A fine miniature developed by the well-known French hybridizer, Francis Meilland, developer of 'Peace'. Free blooming.

CUDDLES

ARS Rating: 8.0   Miniature   Introduced: 1978

Flower: Egg-shaped buds open into high-centered, deep coral-pink blossoms. Double, 1 to 1-1/2 inches with 55 to 60 reflexed petals. Borne singly with one or two small side buds.

Fragrance: Slight.

Form and Foliage: Low, compact and bushy. Covered with small, dark green leaves.

Comments: Easy to grow. Prolific bloomer. Good lasting quality. Long season. Disease resistant. Good cut and exhibition flower. ARS Award of Excellence, 1979.

FIREFALL

ARS Rating: 7.3   Miniature   Introduced: 1980

Flower: Short, rounded buds open into full, bright red blooms. Double, 1/2 to 1 inch with 40 to 50 petals. Flowers borne in clusters.

Fragrance: Slight.

Form and Foliage: Trailing or wide spreading (up to 6 feet) with arching canes. Tiny, very glossy leaves.

Comments: Extremely prolific in spring. Repeats well the rest of the season. Hardy. Unusual downward pointing thorns. Can be used in hanging baskets or as a ground cover.

GREEN ICE

ARS Rating: 7.4   Miniature   Introduced: 1971

Flower: Small, soft pink buds give way to white blooms that change to light green. Double, 1 to 1-1/2 inches with many petals. Borne in small clusters.

Fragrance: None.

Form and Foliage: Trailing and bushy. Small to medium height if trained upward. Vigorous grower. Small, glossy green foliage.

Comments: A most unusual flower color. Easy to grow. Prolific and long lasting. In cool climates the flower will pick up a pinkish tinge. Prefers some shade. Disease resistant. Makes an excellent hanging basket. Good cut and exhibition flower.

HI-HO

ARS Rating: 8.3   Climbing Miniature   Introduced: 1964

Flower: Pointed, deep pink buds open into dainty, coral-rose blooms. Double, 1/2 to 1 inch with many petals. Borne in small clusters.

Fragrance: Slight.

Form and Foliage: Upright, climbs to about 4 feet. Vigorous grower. Glossy green, leathery leaves.

Comments: Excellent climbing miniature. Abundant blooms have long-lasting quality over a long season. Perfect for a low fence. Good cut flower for corsages or boutonnieres. Top exhibition flower.

'Cuddles'

'Green Ice'

'Holy Toledo'

'Kara'

HOLY TOLEDO
Miniature
ARS Rating: 8.5 · Introduced: 1978

Flower: Long, pointed buds give way to outstanding blooms of deep apricot with a yellow base and reverse. Double, 1-1/2 to 2 inches with 25 to 30 petals. Borne singly or in clusters of up to 5.

Fragrance: Slight.

Form and Foliage: Medium to tall and shapely. Vigorous grower. Deep green, glossy foliage.

Comments: Prolific bloomer. Repeats quickly. Long lasting. Sharp thorns. ARS Award of Excellence, 1980.

JEANNE LAJOIE
Climbing Miniature
ARS Rating: 8.0 · Introduced: 1975

Flower: Beautiful hybrid tea-type. Pointed buds give way to reflexed, high-centered blooms of medium pink with a darker underside. Double, 1 to 1-1/2 inches with 35 to 40 petals. Borne in clusters.

Fragrance: Slight.

Form and Foliage: Upright, trailing and bushy. Climbs up to 4 feet high. Vigorous grower. Small, glossy green leaves.

Comments: Profuse blooms all season. Won't fade. Good for hanging baskets or on a trellis. ARS Award of Excellence, 1977.

JUDY FISCHER
Miniature
ARS Rating: 8.8 · Introduced: 1968

Flower: Beautifully formed, hybrid tea-type buds of rose-pink open into clear, rose-pink blooms. Double, 1/2 to 1 inch. Borne singly or in small clusters.

Fragrance: Slight.

Form and Foliage: Low, compact and bushy. Glossy, dark green, leathery leaves have a copper tinge.

Comments: One of the best pink miniatures. Flower lasts for weeks and doesn't fade, even in hot weather. Disease resistant. Good cut flower. Top exhibition rose. ARS Award of Excellence, 1975.

KARA
Miniature (Moss)
ARS Rating: 7.8 · Introduced: 1972

Flower: Tiny, pointed, very mossy buds give way to delightful, single blooms of medium pink with bright yellow stamens 1/2 to 1 inch long with 5 broad petals. Borne in small clusters.

Fragrance: None.

Form and Foliage: Very low and bushy. Abundant, small, green leaves.

Comments: Prolific bloomer all season. Long-lasting flowers. Disease resistant. Does well indoors under lights.

LAVENDER JEWEL

ARS Rating: 8.0
Miniature
Introduced: 1978

Flower: Small, pointed buds open into full, high-centered, soft lavender blooms of excellent form. Double, 1 inch with 35 to 40 petals. Borne singly and in clusters.

Fragrance: Slight.

Form and Foliage: Compact and bushy. Grows vigorously. Glossy, dark green leaves.

Comments: Blooms are produced lavishly over a long season. Attractive, disease-resistant foliage. Good cut flower.

LAVENDER LACE

ARS Rating: 7.6
Miniature
Introduced: 1968

Flower: Small, tea-shaped buds open into classic-shaped, soft lavender blooms. Double, high-centered, about 1-1/2 inches wide. Borne singly and in clusters.

Fragrance: Moderate.

Form and Foliage: Medium height, spreading and compact. Grows vigorously. Small, glossy green leaves.

Comments: The first true lavender miniature. Free blooming and long lasting with an attractive growth habit. Good cut flower. Pleasant fragrance. A favorite grown with artificial lights. ARS Award of Excellence, 1975.

LEMON DELIGHT

ARS Rating: 7.0
Miniature (Moss)
Introduced: 1978

Flower: Long, tapered, mossy buds give way to beautiful, yellow blooms with golden stamens. Semidouble, 1-1/2 inches with 10 petals. Borne in small clusters.

Fragrance: The moss on the buds has a slight lemony scent.

Form and Foliage: Short and bushy. Small, pointed, glossy, dark green leaves.

Comments: Prolific bloomer all season.

MAGIC CARROUSEL

ARS Rating: 8.9
Miniature
Introduced: 1972

Flower: Nicely shaped, long, pointed buds open into small, high-centered, white blooms with red or deep pink edging. Double, 1-1/2 to 2 inches with many petals. Borne singly or in clusters of 2 or 3.

Fragrance: Moderate. Similar to violets.

Form and Foliage: Bushy and fairly tall. Well clothed in glossy bronze foliage.

Comments: Very popular miniature with a gorgeous flower. Continual producer of long-lasting blooms. Relatively thornless. Disease resistant. Good cut flower. Top exhibition rose. ARS Award of Excellence, 1975.

'Lavender Lace'

'Lavender Jewel'

Top: 'Magic Carrousel'. Left: 'Starina'. Right: 'Judy Fischer'. Bottom: 'Mary Marshall'.

MARY MARSHALL
Miniature
ARS Rating: 8.7   Introduced: 1970

Flower: Perfectly pointed, hybrid tea-type buds open into high-centered, coral-orange blooms with yellow bases. Double, 1-3/4 inches, borne in floribunda-like clusters.

Fragrance: Light to moderate.

Form and Foliage: Medium height and bushy. Vigorous grower. Dark green, leathery leaves.

Comments: Great producer of nearly perfect flowers. Excellent cut flower. Top exhibition rose. ARS Award of Excellence, 1975.

MOOD MUSIC
Miniature (Moss)
ARS Rating: 7.0   Introduced: 1977

Flower: Long, heavily mossed buds open into shapely blooms of peach-orange, turning medium pink with age. Double, 1 to 1-1/2 inches with 40 to 50 petals. Borne singly or in clusters.

Fragrance: Moderate.

Form and Foliage: Tall, heavily branched and bushy. Vigorous grower. Abundant amount of semiglossy green leaves.

Comments: Flowers produced continually during the entire season. Profuse. Repeats quickly. Long-lasting buds.

OVER THE RAINBOW
Miniature
ARS Rating: 8.5   Introduced: 1974

Flower: Large, pointed buds quickly open into small, high-centered, hybrid tea-type blooms. Bicolored blooms are red and pink with gold at the base and on the reverse. Double, 1 to 1-1/2 inches with many petals. Borne in clusters.

Fragrance: Slight.

Form and Foliage: Leathery, medium green foliage. Vigorous and bushy.

Comments: Easy to grow. Prolific, with quick repeats. Top exhibition rose. 'Climbing Over the Rainbow' is a popular, 5 to 6-foot sport of the bush form.

PEACHES 'n CREAM
Miniature
ARS Rating: 8.0   Introduced: 1976

Flower: Nicely tapered buds open into luscious peach and pink blended blooms. Double, high-centered, 1 inch wide with 50 to 55 petals. Borne singly and in clusters.

Fragrance: Light.

Form and Foliage: Low and rather spreading. Abundant, dark green foliage.

Comments: Free blooming and long lasting. Good cut flower. Top exhibition rose. ARS Award of Excellence, 1977.

'Peaches 'n Cream'

PINK CAMEO

ARS Rating: 8.4   Climbing Miniature
     Introduced: 1954

Flower: Small buds open into rose-pink blooms with darker centers. Double, 1-1/4 inches with 20 to 25 petals. Borne in large clusters.

Fragrance: Slight.

Form and Foliage: Tall and upright. Small, rich, glossy green leaves.

Comments: Developed by Ralph Moore, it is the first everblooming, climbing miniature. Abundant bloomer. Sometimes classed as a polyantha.

PINK PETTICOAT

ARS Rating: 7.5   Miniature
     Introduced: 1979

Flower: Exquisitely pointed buds open into creamy white, reflexed blooms brushed with deep coral-pink on the outer edges. Double, 1-1/2 to 2 inches with 30 to 35 petals. Borne singly.

Fragrance: Slight.

Form and Foliage: Upright, tall and bushy. Glossy, dark green leaves.

Comments: Prolific. Flowers are long lasting. Beautiful in all stages. Very healthy and robust. Sharp thorns. ARS Award of Excellence, 1980.

POPCORN

ARS Rating: 8.0   Miniature
     Introduced: 1973

Flower: Creamy white buds open into masses of tiny, pure white blooms with buttery yellow stamens. Single, 1/2 to 3/4 inch with 5 petals. Borne in clusters or sprays of 15 to 25 blooms.

Fragrance: Light. Honey scented.

Form and Foliage: Medium height and upright. Vigorous grower. Fernlike, glossy, light green leaves.

Comments: One of the most profuse miniatures. Blooms resemble popcorn. Top exhibition flower.

PUPPY LOVE

ARS Rating: 8.0   Miniature
     Introduced: 1978

Flower: Pointed buds open into high-centered, multicolored blooms of orange, pink and yellow. Double, 1-1/2 inches with 20 to 25 petals. Borne singly on long stems.

Fragrance: Slight.

Form and Foliage: Medium height, upright and compact. Medium green leaves.

Comments: Free blooming with excellent flower form. Good cut or exhibition flower. ARS Award of Excellence, 1979.

'Popcorn'

'Puppy Love'

'Red Cascade'

'Rise 'n Shine'

RED CASCADE
ARS Rating: 7.5

Climbing Miniature
Introduced: 1976

Flower: Small, pointed buds open into dark red, cup-shaped blooms. Double, 3/4 to 1 inch with 45 to 60 petals. Borne in clusters.

Fragrance: None.

Form and Foliage: Versatile form. Described as prostrate, arching, spreading, bushy and dense. Main stems reach 4 to 6 feet high and spread up to 5 feet wide. Abundant, small, leathery leaves.

Comments: A versatile landscape rose. Use as ground cover, for pillars, in hanging baskets or to climb up anything. Extremely profuse and long lasting. Strong canes. Can be a bit difficult to grow and is subject to mildew. Must be established a year before it blooms heavily. ARS Award of Excellence, 1976.

RED FLUSH
ARS Rating: 7.0

Miniature
Introduced: 1978

Flower: Egg-shaped buds open into light to medium red, cup-shaped blooms. Double, 1-1/2 inch with 50 to 60 petals. Borne singly or in clusters.

Fragrance: None.

Form and Foliage: Low to medium height, compact and bushy. Attractively serrated, glossy green leaves.

Comments: Produces great waves of blossoms. Stands up well in all weather and repeats quickly. Susceptible to mildew. ARS Award of Excellence, 1979.

RED IMP
ARS Rating: 7.7

Miniature
Introduced: 1951

Flower: Deep red, egg-shaped buds give way to well-formed, deep crimson blooms. Double, 3/4 to 1 inch with 45 to 55 tightly packed petals.

Fragrance: Slight.

Form and Foliage: Small, bushy and heavily branched. Small, dark green leaves.

Comments: Very popular miniature. Produces an abundance of unfading, long-lasting flowers. Ideal for containers.

RISE 'n SHINE
ARS Rating: 8.5

Miniature
Introduced: 1977

Flower: Long, pointed buds unfold into rich, brilliant yellow blooms. Double, 1-1/2 inches with 30 to 40 petals. Borne singly and in clusters.

Fragrance: Light.

Form and Foliage: Beautifully compact, bushy and low. Vigorous grower. Dark green leaves.

Comments: One of the finest yellow miniatures. Prolific and continuous. Attractive bush. ARS Award of Excellence, 1978.

SHERI ANNE
ARS Rating: 8.0   Miniature   Introduced: 1973

Flower: Long, pointed buds become bright orange-red blooms. Semidouble, 1 to 1-1/2 inches with 15 to 18 petals. Borne singly and in clusters.

Fragrance: Light.

Form and Foliage: Medium to tall, upright and bushy. Glossy, dark green, leathery leaves.

Comments: Profuse and continuous. Good cut and exhibition flower. ARS Award of Excellence, 1975.

'Sheri Anne'

STARINA
ARS Rating: 9.4   Miniature   Introduced: 1965

Flower: Hybrid tea-type buds open into luminous orange-red blooms with yellow bases. Double, 1-1/2 to 2 inches and borne singly and in clusters.

Fragrance: Slight.

Form and Foliage: Excellent form—low and compact. Glossy, dark green leaves.

Comments: Probably the most adored of all miniature roses. Winner of more American and international awards than any other miniature. Has highest ARS rating of any rose. One of only 10 roses rated higher than 9.0. Perfectly formed flowers. Abundant blooms over long season. Excellent cut flower and top exhibition rose.

'Starina'

TOY CLOWN
ARS Rating: 8.9   Miniature   Introduced: 1966

Flower: Beautiful, hybrid tea-type buds open into white blooms edged in deep pink or red. Semidouble, 1-1/2 inches with 20 to 25 petals. Borne singly and in clusters.

Fragrance: Slight.

Form and Foliage: Medium height, moderately compact and vigorous. Small to medium sized leaves, medium green and leathery.

Comments: A good landscape miniature with a very free bloom and attractive habit. Gold Certificate, 1971; ARS Award of Excellence, 1975.

'Yellow Doll'

YELLOW DOLL
ARS Rating: 8.3   Miniature   Introduced: 1962

Flower: Slender, pointed buds open into clear yellow blossoms. Double, 1-1/2 inches with 50 to 60 narrow petals. Borne singly and in clusters.

Fragrance: Moderate.

Form and Foliage: Low and compact. Vigorous grower. Deep green, leathery foliage.

Comments: A very popular yellow miniature with attractive form and abundant bloom.

Tree and Shrub Roses

Tree roses are actually three different kinds of roses, all grafted into one. There is the *rootstock,* the *trunkstock* or *standard,* and the flowering *top part.* Their effect in the garden can be dramatic, lending an air of formality. But because of the effort and time required to make them, they are more expensive. The top graft union is also sensitive to cold, so tree roses are not very hardy.

Different forms—Any kind of rose may be grafted to the trunkstock. Weeping standards are very popular in England. They are made with the soft-caned ramblers which sometimes drape all the way to the ground. In the United States, more upright growing roses are preferred. Even these have different shapes and sizes.

'Bewitched' and 'Queen Elizabeth' make very tall, vigorous, upright growing standards, almost the size of a small specimen tree. They are two of the largest. 'King's Ransom', 'Mister Lincoln' and 'Chrysler Imperial' are also vigorous and upright, but not quite as tall.

'Peace', 'Chicago Peace' and 'Tropicana' are tall and vigorous, but instead of being upright, they make spreading, rounded "trees."

'Pink Peace', 'Electron', 'Fragrant Cloud' and 'Double Delight' are hybrid teas that make dense, bushy flowering heads.

Popular grandifloras for tree roses are 'Olé', 'Pink Parfait' and 'Prominent'. They make rather small, dense heads that produce many flowers.

Low-growing floribundas make excellent tree roses, or 2-foot high "patio" standards. 'Sarabande' is compact and very attractive. Others frequently available are 'Angel Face', 'Cherish', 'Charisma' and 'Europeana'.

Culture—Sun is the enemy of the trunkstock and it is very important to protect trunks in some way. Tree roses are planted with a support stake and that stake should be placed on the hotter south or west-facing side. The trunk should also be painted white with water-base paint, or wrapped. If the trunk is seared by the sun, it will split and become susceptible to borer attack.

Where winter temperatures dip to 10° F (−12° C) and below, some kind of cold protection is necessary.

Top, left to right: 'Queen Elizabeth', 'Olé' and 'Europeana'. Center: Space tree roses the same as bush roses, about 3 feet apart. Bottom left: 'Renae', a climbing floribunda, makes a *bona fide* "tree" rose when grafted to a trunkstock. Bottom right: 'Margo Koster', a polyantha, as a tree rose.

Harison's Yellow.

Plants should be tightly wrapped all the way to the top. For more protection, partially uproot the bush, lay it on its side and cover with soil.

SHRUB ROSES

The shrub roses include many roses which do not fit neatly into other categories. Consequently, it is quite a varied group of plants. Some shrub roses are centuries old and have been important in the development of today's modern roses. Others are modern roses, the result of extensive breeding programs.

Because they are a varied group, shrub roses have a lot to offer. Most of them are superb landscape plants with unmatched versatility. They make excellent hedges and screens. With proper training, some can be used as ground covers and many have climbing habits perfectly suited to trellises, arbors or fences.

Many shrub roses have a natural beauty all their own which cannot be found in more popular types of roses. A large number have bright red hips in fall and winter, some have blossoms that are uniquely fragrant. All are beautiful.

In general, shrub roses are tough, low-maintenance plants. Many are very hardy and thrive well outside normal rose growing areas. Pruning is kept to a minimum and usually consists of removing dead wood and criss-crossing branches. Most shrub roses are also relatively disease resistant.

The blossoms of shrub roses are single or multi-petaled and come in many colors. Some bloom only once in spring or early summer. Others bloom throughout the summer and into fall. Most bloom prolifically.

The following are some popular shrub roses:

'Frühlingsgold'—Also known as 'Spring Gold'. Orange-red buds open into single, golden yellow blossoms. Flowers are 2 to 3 inches in diameter, have 7 petals and a strong fragrance. Growth is vigorous to 6 to 10 feet. Leaves are wrinkled and soft green. Blooms once in late spring.

'Frühlingsmorgen'—Single, reddish pink blossoms have soft, yellow centers and maroon stamens. Flowers are 3 to 4 inches in diameter and have 5 to 7 petals. Fragrance is moderate. Growth is 5 to 7 feet high. Blooms occur mainly in spring but often again in fall and develop into large red hips.

'Golden Wings'—Large, single, sulfur yellow blossoms are 4 to 5 inches in diameter, have 5 to 7 petals. Blossoms produce light fragrance. Vigorous and very hardy. Grows 4 to 6 feet high and blooms prolifically in late spring and again in fall.

***Rosa harisonii*, Harison's Yellow**—Small, semidouble, bright yellow flowers are 1-1/2 to 2 inches in diameter with 10 to 14 petals and strong fragrance. Foliage is rich green. Plants reach 5 to 7 feet in height. Blooms prolifically in late spring.

'Nevada'—Large, pink buds open into single, white blossoms often splashed with red on the backsides. Flowers are 4 to 5 inches in diameter and have 5 to 7 petals of slight fragrance. Grows 5 to 8 feet in height with light green leaves and few thorns. Blooms prolifically in spring and fall.

'Poulsen's Park Rose'—Large, 4 to 5-inch double silvery pink blossoms have excellent form and slight fragrance. Grows vigorously to 3 to 6 feet in height with a wide, spreading habit. Blooms continuously.

'Sea Foam'—Double, creamy white flowers borne in clusters. Blooms in spring and fall. Glossy green foliage. Vigorous trailing habit. Good choice for a ground cover.

'Sparrieshoop'—Single, light pink blooms, 3 to 4 inches in diameter with 7 petals and strong fragrance. Leathery foliage. Vigorous upright growth to 12 feet. Blooms in spring and fall.

'Thérèse Bugnet'—Deep red buds open into double, 4-inch blossoms colored red fading to pink blossoms. Fragrance is strong. Grows 5 to 6 feet high and blooms in spring and fall.

SPECIES ROSES

***Rosa banksiae*, Lady Banks' Rose**—White or yellow slightly fragrant flowers are about 1 inch in diameter. They appear in large clusters in May to June. Foliage is evergreen. The plant will climb to 20 feet or more. Most popular are double forms 'Alba-plena' and 'Lutea'.

Rosa banksiae 'Lutea'

'Pink Grootendorst'

'Blanc Double de Coubert'

'Sparrieshoop'

Rosa foetida Bicolor, **Austrian Copper**—Scarlet-orange, 2 to 3-inch single blossoms have yellow backsides. Fragrance is unusual. Grows 4 to 6 feet in height, blooms once in spring and is very hardy. Famous as the genetic source of yellow, salmon and apricot-colored modern roses.

Rosa hugonis, **Father Hugo's Rose or Golden Rose of China**—Single, light yellow flowers, 1-1/2 to 2 inches in diameter with 5 to 7 petals and slight fragrance. Grows 6 to 8 feet high with gracefully arching branches.

Rosa eglanteria, **Sweet Brier or Eglantine Rose**—Often referred to as one of England's most treasured wild plants. Clear pink, semidouble flowers are borne on an arching bush that generally reaches about 8 feet high. Both flower and foliage have apple-like fragrance. Widely used in breeding.

Rosa moyesii—Single blossoms are a blend of deep blood red and pink. Flowers are 1-1/2 to 2-1/2 inches in diameter, have 5 petals and a slight fragrance. Hips are bright orange-red. Grows up to 10 feet high and blooms in late spring.

ROSA RUGOSA HYBRIDS AND VARIETIES

The species and its hybrids make up an important group of shrub roses. In general, they are very hardy, have crinkled, shiny, dark green leaves, bright red or orange-red hips and fragrant flowers. Plants usually grow 4 to 7 feet high.

The species has single, purplish red flowers, 2-1/2 to 3-1/2 inches in diameter with 5 to 7 petals. It reaches 5 to 6 feet in height and blooms in spring and fall.

'Blanc Double de Coubert'—Large, very fragrant, double white flowers with yellow stamens. Blooms both spring and fall and reaches 4 to 7 feet in height.

'F.J. Grootendorst'—Small, double, crimson-red flowers borne in clusters. Petals are ruffled and give the flower a carnation-like appearance. Slight fragrance. Makes an excellent hedge. 'Grootendorst Supreme' has deeper crimson-red flowers and 'Pink Grootendorst' has ruffled pink blossoms.

'Frau Dagmar Hartopp'—Produces a profusion of beautiful, silvery pink single blossoms 2 to 3 inches in diameter. Bright yellow stamens. Low growing, compact habit ideal for a hedge.

'Hansa'—Large, double, reddish violet blossoms are 3 to 4 inches in diameter and produce a wonderfully strong clove-like aroma. Very free blooming on weak stems. Large red hips.

Rosa rugosa rosea—Light pink, single flowers 2 to 3 inches in diameter with 5 to 7 petals. Grows 5 to 7 feet high and blooms in spring and fall.

Rosa rugosa rubra—Similar to *R. rugosa* but with wine crimson blossoms and creamy yellow stamens.

'Sarah Van Fleet'—Continuous production of medium pink, semidouble blossoms, 4 to 5 inches in diameter. Blossoms have 20 petals with a strong fragrance. Can grow as high as 10 feet but is normally compact.

'Schneezwerg'—Also known as 'Snowdwarf', this rose has beautiful, snow white, semidouble flowers with yellow stamens. Blossoms are 1 to 2 inches in diameter and have at most 20 petals of slight fragrance. Borne in clusters of 3 to 10. Grows 3 to 4 feet high and blooms in spring and fall.

KORDESII SHRUBS

Kordesii shrubs were developed by the reknowned German hybridizer, Wilhelm Kordes. He concentrated on sweet briers and rugosas and the climber 'Dortmund' is one of his most popular varieties. In general, Kordesii shrubs are very hardy and easy to grow. Listed below are a few other valuable Kordesii roses.

'Berlin'—A hybrid of 'Eva' and 'Peace' producing large, single, orange-scarlet blossoms with gold centers. Borne in clusters. Upright and very vigorous to 5 to 6 feet high. Dark green leaves.

'Bonn'—Large, double, orange-red blossoms have a musk-like fragrance. They are 4 inches in diameter with 25 petals. Glossy foliage. Grows 4 to 5 feet high.

'Elmshorn'—Small, double, deep pink blossoms borne in large clusters are 1 inch in diameter with 20 petals. Blossoms have a slight fragrance. Light green, wrinkled leaves. Free blooming.

'Erfurt'—Very large, semidouble, bright yellow blooms are edged in red. Plants grow vigorously with a trailing habit. Blooms in spring and fall.

HARDY BUCK ROSES

Professor Griffith Buck of Iowa State University has developed a group of hardy, carefree, shrub roses which are increasing in popularity.

'Applejack'—Large, semidouble, bright pink flowers are 3 to 4 inches in diameter. Grows vigorously to 5 feet. Blooms in spring and fall. Apple scented foliage.

'Prairie Flower'—Single, carmine-red blossoms are 2 to 3 inches in diameter with 6 to 8 petals and light fragrance. Plants grow to about 4 feet high. Continuous bloom.

'Square Dancer'—Large, double, rose-pink blossoms borne in clusters of 4 to 5. Petals flare out wide like a swirling skirt to reveal bright yellow stamens. Plants grow 4 feet high. Blooms continuously.

Other Buck roses worth considering include deep pink 'Country Dancer', light rose 'Carefree Beauty' and pink and white bicolored 'Prairie Star'.

The Rosarian's Rose

A rosarian is anyone who has a fine appreciation of roses. A lifetime of experience is not required and neither is membership in any organization. But most individuals who call themselves *rosarians* are members of a local rose society.

The American Rose Society sponsors a network of "pro" rosarians, officially called *Consulting Rosarians*. Consulting Rosarians are appointed by the ARS district directors to help fellow rose lovers grow better roses. And you don't have to be an ARS member to consult with these experts. Sound promising? Just write to the ARS (P.O. Box 30,000, Shreveport, LA 71130) and ask about a garden consultation. They will refer you to the nearest Consulting Rosarian.

All rosarians, consulting or otherwise, do share certain traits. The majority are dedicated to or perhaps even a bit compulsive about roses. They have plenty of topics to explore: new varieties, new cultural methods and new colors. There is always plenty of grist for the rose lover's mill.

There are more than 360 affiliated and associated local rose societies in the United States. One of the major activities of the local societies is the exhibition of roses, and many rosarians participate.

EXHIBITING ROSES

The competitive urge coupled with love of a beautiful rose is likely the primary motivation of rose exhibitors. At shows you can see roses grown to perfection, looking better than in the most promising catalog.

At a show, you may be shocked to see a near-perfect specimen of a rose you grow. In your garden it seems nice but is not nearly as beautiful. Don't be alarmed; this is a common experience. The greatest service of the rosarian-exhibitor is providing a good example. With dedication and purpose, the rosarian uses the very latest rose-growing know-how. Seeking the optimum potential of the flower, they produce feasts for our eyes and show us the way to success.

Rose shows are not for experts only. There is no better way for the amateur to see what a well grown rose looks like.

The garden of a rose exhibitor does not look much different than any other. But most of Bill Hillman's roses have produced award winning roses. In the foreground is 'White Christmas'. Some years back, Bill won Queen of the Show with it. The pink rose is 'Queen Elizabeth', a great show rose since its introduction in 1954.

Planning to exhibit roses begins with your choices of which roses to grow. Take a look at the list of top exhibition roses beginning on page 54. These are roses that win the most awards. Or, attend local society meetings. Ask some questions and you'll get an earful of good advice—what to plant, how to prune, proper timing. Either source of advice represents years of accumulated experience you would be wise to take advantage of.

The following will guide you through the basic steps in preparing roses for exhibition.

EARLY PLANNING

The hybrid teas 'First Prize' and 'Pristine' are two varieties that win many awards. Of course you can also show grandifloras, floribundas, miniatures, old roses and shrub roses. Be prepared to follow the principles of rose culture closely—water, feed, prune and protect.

PRUNING

When to prune is important. If you prune too early, flowering will peak before the show. Prune too late and you'll have too few blooms to choose from. The time between pruning and flowering varies according to climate, but it's usually 1-1/2 to 2 months. You can save time by simply asking a more experienced exhibitor in your area about the best time to prune. Then prune your bushes a few at a time, beginning one week before the best date, and continuing up to one week after.

Pruning for exhibition is similar to normal pruning, (page 37), but it's directed towards concentrating the plant's energy into fewer flowers. Experts "thumb prune." This means removing all but about four buds per cane by rubbing them off with your thumb. If there are multiple buds—more than one bud at the same point—keep only the largest.

SPRAYING

Follow your regular spray program until buds begin to show color. Spraying at that time may damage petals. A full complement of healthy leaves is the source of the flower's energy.

WATERING

Supply plenty of water; you can hardly give roses too much. Plenty of water is especially important just before the show. The week before the show, water every day to ensure that the petals develop full substance.

Bob Cowden, Consulting Rosarian and judge, appraises climbing rose flower sprays with an interested audience.

Exhibition Quality Rose

At this Portland Rose Society spring show, the roses are arranged by class and color. Above: Medium red hybrid teas are in front of dark red hybrid teas. Below: The winners' table.

Form	25
Substance	15
Color	20
Size	10
Stem and Foliage	20
Balance and Proportion	10
	100

'Honor', top 1980 ARS All-America rose.

An exhibition-quality hybrid tea or single grandiflora has ample petals, symmetrically arranged in a circular outline. Most important is form, followed by color, stem and substance. Floribunda sprays should show a group of florets on one main or lateral stem. They are judged by the whole spray, which should be of a circular shape with more than one open bloom. Ideally, the spray should show the cycle of bloom. Grandiflora sprays should contain blooms at the same stage of development. The individual blooms are considered, as well as to the overall appearance of the spray. Most important—judges look first at the overall beauty of the rose, not its faults.

DISBUDDING

Hybrid teas and single grandifloras must be shown disbudded. This means that all buds, except the large one that will become the flower, should be removed as soon as you see them. The sooner you do this the better. You can disbud on the day of the show, but your flower will lose points for the wounds. Usually there will be at least one extra bud, although some varieties normally produce more. See page 40.

SHADING

Flowers of many varieties will be improved if opening buds are given some protection from sun and rain. Either a simple, homemade shade device or a commercial protection cone can be used. Wait until the petals have begun to open before installing a shade device.

CUTTING FOR SHOW

Naturally, you would like to have all your best roses in full flower the night before the show. But things rarely work out so smoothly. So, cut when you think the flower is ready, whether morning, noon or night, one to three days before the show. Blooms with unfolded sepals are about three days away from being "show ready."

Get to know your roses—which flowers open fast and which open slowly. Generally, flowers with fewer petals open faster. If you want to cut this type of rose a few days before the show, do it while the bud is still fairly tight, but when the sepals open. If the weather is hot, cut flowers while they are still tight in the bud. Naturally, thick-petaled flowers will last longest. Keep a diary and you'll quickly learn the best times to cut your roses.

Have a bucket of water right in the garden with you for the cut roses. Leave stems as long as you can because you'll need to trim them later. If you cut the night before the show, simply leave the roses immersed in the bucket to their necks in a 35° F (2° C) refrigerator. Roses will keep for four or five days. A tray of water will increase humidity. Remove apples or other ripening fruit from the refrigerator. They will speed up the blooming process.

After cutting in the garden, clean the leaves with a mild soap solution and dry them. Arrange them for storage or transportation so they will not damage each other. Give each rose a name tag.

Straightening bent necks. Immerse the entire flower in tepid, 100° F (37° C) water and trim an inch of stem from the base. Straighten the neck while it's under-water and leave submerged for another 20 minutes or so. It will be upright with a straight neck after this treatment.

TRANSPORTATION
Keep the roses in water if possible. If not, damp newspaper or cloth will help. Separate them with crumpled paper to prevent damage. Travel early. The air will be cooler and you'll have more time to set up at the show.

AT THE SHOW
It's a good idea to carry some grooming tools like cotton swabs and pruning shears. Cut another inch or so from the stem base to improve water absorption. The stem should reach to the bottom of the vase. Set too high, the flower may run out of water and droop before judging time.

Fill out entry tags completely and accurately. Attach them to vases. Double check the show schedule to make sure of the classes you can enter. Keep your own records—entering two flowers of the same variety in the same class will disqualify both.

Give the flowers one last grooming. Look for dust specks on the petals. Upon presentation, the rose should look as natural as possible.

Making Cut Roses Last

'Jack O' Lantern'

The ideal time for cutting roses is between 3 and 5 p.m. when leaves and flowers have their most abundant food supply and can continue to do well for a longer time.

A sharp knife or scissors-type pruning shears are the best for cutting roses. Do not crush or mash the stem. This will injure the conducting tissue and prevent the movement of water up the stem.

The growth stage of the bud is important. Much depends on the variety, and, to some degree, on climatic conditions. Varieties with few petals should be cut "tight," even before the green sepals unfold. Roses with 40 or more petals should be cut after a few petals have unfolded.

Once the roses are cut, immerse them in a deep container of warm water for about 20 minutes. This treatment will also straighten bent necks and revive wilted roses. Then move them to a cool, dark place for one or two hours. Before arranging, wash leaves and stems with warm, soapy water.

If the roses are placed in water immediately and then removed later, trim about an inch from the base after replacing them in water. The cutting must be done underwater, because air is sucked into the stem instantly.

When possible, it helps to change the water and to make a fresh, slanting cut in the stems (1/2 inch back) daily or at least every other day. Also, if you can, place the arrangement in a cool spot at night.

Materials designed to prolong the life of cut flowers have been used for many years. Most of the current cut flower preservatives seek to prevent bacterial decay of the stems. Preservatives make a vase of cut roses last 5 to 7 days longer. Using preservatives with all the steps outlined above will add 10 days or more to the life of some cut roses.

New Roses

Dozens of roses are introduced each year, but only a select few receive the acclaim of accomplished rose gardeners. The following are outstanding new roses introduced since 1981, many of which are All-America Rose Selections.

BRANDY
Hybrid Tea

ARS Rating: 7.5   Introduced: 1981   AARS 1982

Flower: Large, long, tapered buds open into beautiful apricot blossoms. Classically formed, double, 4 to 5-1/2 inches with 30 broad petals.

Fragrance: Moderate tea scent.

Form and Foliage: Medium height, strong and bushy. Large, semiglossy leaves.

Comments: Hybrid of 'First Prize' and 'Golden Wave'. Has classic flower form of 'First Prize'. Good disease resistance. Fine cut flower.

FRENCH LACE
Floribunda

ARS Rating: 8.0   Introduced: 1981   AARS 1982

Flower: Large, pointed, ivory to apricot buds swirl open into exquisite ivory blooms of hybrid tea quality. Double, 4 to 5 inches. Borne in clusters of eight or more.

Fragrance: Light. Spicy.

Form and Foliage: Vigorous, well-branched plant of medium height. Dense, dark green foliage.

Comments: An excellent floribunda that produces classic flowers over a long period. Picks up a pink tinge in cool climates. Disease resistant. Good cut flower.

GOLD MEDAL
Grandiflora

ARS Rating: _____ Introduced: 1982

Flower: Long, pointed, deep gold buds touched with orange-red open into long-lasting blooms. Double, 3-1/2 to 4-1/2 inches with 35 to 40 broad, stiff petals.

Fragrance: Moderate.

Form and Foliage: Tall, vigorous plant. Large, glossy, deep green leaves.

Comments: Hardy.

GRAND MASTERPIECE
Hybrid Tea

ARS Rating: _____ Introduced: 1984

Flower: Long-pointed, deep red buds open into beautifully formed, high-centered, rich red blossoms on strong stems. Double, 4 inches with 30 to 35 petals.

Fragrance: Mild.

Form and Foliage: Vigorous growing, tall plant. Medium green foliage.

Comments: Long-lasting cut flower. Tall for a hybrid tea. Requires careful pruning.

IMPATIENT

ARS Rating: _____   Floribunda
Introduced: 1983   AARS 1984

Flower: Large, brilliant orange-red blooms. Double, 3 inches with 20 to 25 petals. Borne in clusters on long, strong stems.

Fragrance: Mild.

Form and Foliage: Tall, upright plant. Densely covered with dark, shiny green foliage.

Comments: Tall for a floribunda. Blooms continually. Good disease resistance.

INTRIGUE

ARS Rating: _____   Floribunda
Introduced: 1983   AARS 1984

Flower: Large, blackish purple, globular buds open into rich, deep plum-colored blooms. Double, 3 inches. Borne in small clusters.

Fragrance: Strong old rose fragrance. Lemony.

Form and Foliage: Upright, medium habit. Glossy, clean green foliage.

Comments: Disease resistant.

JENNIFER HART
ARS Rating: _____

Hybrid Tea
Introduced: 1983

Flower: Ovoid-pointed, blood-red buds open into deep red blooms, often marked with blackish red. Double, 4-1/2 to 5 inches with 40 to 50 petals. Long, strong stems.

Fragrance: Moderate.

Form and Foliage: Medium-size, vigorous plant. Dark green foliage.

Comments: Good cut flower.

MON CHERI
ARS Rating: 7.6

Hybrid Tea
Introduced: 1981   AARS 1982

Flower: Plump, pointed buds open soft pink and gradually turn velvety red. Double, 4-1/2 to 5-1/2 inches with 35 to 40 broad petals.

Fragrance: Moderate.

Form and Foliage: Short, well-rounded, bushy plant. Dark green, semiglossy foliage.

Comments: Flower is actually a red blend with varying amounts of pink edging depending on amount of light and heat plant receives. Similar to 'Double Delight', which is one parent. Deeper red with full sun and high temperatures. Disease resistant. Good cut flower.

OLYMPIAD

Hybrid Tea

ARS Rating:    Introduced: 1983   AARS 1984

Flower: Large, long-lasting, crimson blooms. Double, 4 to 5 inches. Borne singly or in clusters on long, strong stems.

Fragrance: Moderate.

Form and Foliage: Medium height. Dense, medium green leaves.

Comments: Official rose of the 1984 Olympics. Excellent cut flower. Good disease resistance and hardiness.

SHOWBIZ

Floribunda

ARS Rating: _____   Introduced: 1984   AARS 1985

Flower: Scarlet-red buds open into large scarlet-red blooms. Semidouble, 2-1/2 to 3 inches with 28 to 30 petals. Borne in clusters.

Fragrance: Slight.

Form and Foliage: Compact, broad plant of medium height. Dense, glossy, dark green foliage.

Comments: Produces masses of blooms continually over a long season. Excellent landscape rose. Good disease resistance. Won many awards in Europe under the name 'Ingrid Weibull'.

SHREVEPORT
Grandiflora

ARS Rating: 7.6   Introduced: 1981   AARS 1982

Flower: Medium, bicolored blossoms suffused with orange, salmon, cream and yellow tones. Double, 3 to 4 inches with 45 to 55 crisp petals. Strong stems. Borne in clusters.

Fragrance: Mild tea scent.

Form and Foliage: Tall, bushy, upright plant. Dark green foliage.

Comments: Named for the city that serves as headquarters for the American Rose Society. Easy to grow, disease resistant. Good cut flower.

SUNBRIGHT
Hybrid Tea

ARS Rating: ————   Introduced: 1984

Flower: Long, urn-shaped, deep yellow buds spiral open into large, bright yellow blooms. Double, 4-1/2 to 5-1/2 inches with 24 to 30 petals. Strong stems. Borne singly and in clusters.

Fragrance: Slight.

Form and Foliage: Tall, vigorous plant. Glossy, dark green leaves.

Comments: Long-lasting blooms in hot or cool weather. Blooms over a long season. Good cut flower.

SUN FLARE

Floribunda

ARS Rating: _____   Introduced: 1982   AARS 1983

Flower: Nicely formed, medium, clear lemon yellow blooms. Semidouble, 3 inches. Borne in clusters of 3 to 12.

Fragrance: Mild licorice scent.

Form and Foliage: Vigorous and low growing with a somewhat spreading habit. Glossy green foliage.

Comments: Excellent landscape plant. Disease resistant.

SWEET SURRENDER

Hybrid Tea

ARS Rating: _____   Introduced: 1982   AARS 1983

Flower: Medium, high-centered buds open into clear, silvery pink blooms with beautiful shape. Double, 4-1/2 to 5-1/2 inches. Borne singly on long, tall stems.

Fragrance: Strong.

Form and Foliage: Well-shaped, upright plants with attractive form. Handsome, deep green, leathery leaves.

Comments: Good cut flower.

TRIBUTE

Hybrid Tea

ARS Rating: _____   Introduced: 1983

Flower: Long, rose-red buds swirl open into glowing cerise blooms. Double, 5-inch blooms. Long, strong stems.

Fragrance: Moderate.

Form and Foliage: Tall, vigorous plant. Glossy, dark green foliage.

Comments: Continual bloomer. Excellent cut flower. Good disease resistance.

Dedicated to the Rose

The American Rose Center, operated by the American Rose Society (ARS), is the spiritual and nerve center of rosarians. It contains more than 118 acres of woodland just outside Shreveport, Louisiana. The entire center is a huge test and demonstration garden—some 10,000 roses bloom in more than 35 separate rose gardens. All types of roses are on display in every kind of landscape.

The center is also the source of the *American Rose Magazine* and the *American Rose Annual,* the voice of American rosarians. Subscriptions to both are included with membership in the ARS.

One of the most useful ARS publications is the *Handbook for Selecting Roses.* It is the result of a membership survey that rates all roses currently available. (Also called "Proof of the Pudding." See page 47.) You'll find this numerical rating listed with each rose in this book. The *Handbook for Selecting Roses* is available from the ARS. Send 25¢ and a stamped, self-addressed envelope to:

American Rose Society
P.O. Box 30,000
Shreveport, LA 71130

The ARS provides many other useful services, including sponsorship of many university research programs, Consulting Rosarians (page 153), rose show judge training and an extensive lending library of rose books and films.

Supported by more than 36,000 members nationwide, the American Rose Society is one of the largest and most active of all plant societies.

The international rose—Admiration of the rose does not end at the United States borders. There are many national rose societies and perhaps thousands of local rose societies around the world. England's Royal National Rose Society, established in 1876, was first. The American and Australian societies followed shortly thereafter. All national rose societies (see below) are united by the recently formed World Federation of Rose Societies.

Windsound Carillon Towers at American Rose Center.

The Canadian Rose Society
Mrs. Bey Hunter
20 Portico Drive
Scarborough, Ontario
Canada M1G 3R3

Royal National Rose Society
L. G. Turner
Chiswell Green Lane
St. Albans
Hertfordshire, England

Japan Rose Society
4 - 12 - 6, Todoroki
Setagaya - ku
Tokyo, Japan

Rose Society of South Africa
Ludwig Taschner
Posbus 28188
0132 Sunnyside
Pretoria, South Africa

National Rose Society of New Zealand
Mrs. Heather MacDonanell, Secretary
17 Erin Street
Palmerston, North, New Zealand

Associazione Italiana Della Rosa
Niso Sumagalli
Villa Realle
Monza, Italy

National Rose Society of Australia
Dr. A. S. Thomas
340 Union Road
Dalwyn
Victoria 3103, Australia

Dr. B. Choudhury, Head
Division of Horticulture
Indian Agriculture Research Institute
New Deli 12, India

Dr. Gerd Krussmann
Feldstrasse 9
4902 Bad Salzuslen 1, West Germany

Mr. J. Gaperriere
Route Nationale 6 Chesnes
38 Saint-Quentin-Fallavier, France

Ciopora
Paul Pekmez
2 bis, Route d'Oberhausbergen
67200 Strasbourg, France

Public Rose Gardens

If you are interested in learning about roses, you may want to visit the public rose gardens in your area. There you can see, touch and smell most contemporary roses, and many of the older, hard-to-find varieties. Roses will usually be properly labeled, and a staff horticulturalist is often available to answer questions.

ALABAMA
Battleship Memorial Park
Battleship Memorial Parkway, Mobile

Springdale Plaza Park of Roses
Airport Blvd., Mobile

Bellingrath Gardens, Theodore

ARIZONA
Randolph Park Rose Garden
900 South Randolph Way, Tucson

CALIFORNIA
Arcadia County Park Garden
405 So. Santa Anita Drive, Arcadia

Berkeley Municipal Rose Garden
Euclid Avenue and Eunice, Berkeley

Fresno Municipal Rose Garden
Roeding Park, 890 W. Belmont, Fresno

Descanso Gardens
1418 Descanso Drive, La Canada

Exposition Park Rose Garden
701 State Drive, Los Angeles

Morcom Amphitheatre of Roses
Head of Jean Street off Grand Ave.,
Oakland

Wrigley Estate Rose Garden
391 S. Orange Grove Blvd., Pasadena

Ellis Kindig Memorial Rose Garden
Fairmont Park
2225 Market Street, Riverside

Capitol Park Rose Garden
15th St. & Capitol Ave., Sacramento

Inez Parker Garden at Balboa Park
Park Blvd. at Plaza de Balboa, San Diego

San Jose Municipal Rose Garden
Naglee & Dana Ave., San Jose

Golden Gate Park Rose Garden
J. F. Kennedy Drive, San Francisco

Huntington Botanical Gardens
1151 Oxford Road, San Marino

City Rose Garden
Los Olivos & Laguna Sts., Santa Barbara

Visalia Rose Garden
Tulare County Civic Center, Visalia

Westminster Civic Center
8200 Westminster Avenue, Westminster

✳ Pageant of Roses Garden
Rose Hills Memorial Park
3900 Workman Mill Road, Whittier

COLORADO
Roosevelt Park Rose Garden
8th Ave. & Bross St., Longmont

CONNECTICUT
Norwich Memorial Rose Garden
200 Rockwell Street, Norwich

Hamilton Park Rose Garden
Plank Road, Waterbury

✳ Elizabeth Park Rose Garden
160 Walbridge Rd., W. Hartford

FLORIDA
✳ Florida Cypress Gardens
Cypress Gardens

GEORGIA
Greater Atlanta Rose Garden
Piedmont Park, Atlanta

Thomasville Rose Test Garden
1840 Smith Ave., Thomasville

HAWAII
Queen Kapiolani Park
Paki and Monsarrat, Honolulu

ILLINOIS
Merrick Park Rose Garden
1422 Oak Ave, Evanston

Cook Memorial Park Garden
413 N. Milwaukee Ave., Libertyville

Glen Oak Park Rose Garden
2218 North Prospect Road, Peoria

Robert R. McCormick Memorial Gardens
Cantigny
Roosevelt & Winfield Road, Wheaton

INDIANA
✳ Lakeside Park Rose Garden
1500 Lake Avenue, Fort Wayne

E. G. Hill Memorial Rose Garden
Glen Miller Park, Richmond

IOWA
Iowa State Univ. Rose Garden
Horticultural Gardens, Ames

Bettendorf Park Rose Garden
2204 Grant Street, Bettendorf

Huston Park Rose Garden
3rd Ave. & 15th St., S. E., Cedar Rapids

Vander Veer Park Rose Garden
214 W. Central Park Ave., Davenport

Greenwood Park Rose Garden
4812 Grand Ave., Des Moines

Weed Park Memorial Rose Garden
Muscatine

Iowa Rose Society Garden
Old Highway 30, State Center

KANSAS
✳ E. F. A. Reinisch Rose Garden
Gage Park, Topeka

LOUISIANA
L.S.U. Rose Test Garden
Burden Research Plantation
Essen Lane, Baton Rouge

Hodges Gardens
Highway 171 South, Many

Worthington Memorial Rose Garden
City Park, New Orleans

The American Rose Center
Jefferson-Paige Road, Shreveport

MAINE
Deering Oaks Park Rose Circle
Portland

MARYLAND
Brookside Gardens Rose Garden
1500 Glenallan Ave., Wheaton

MASSACHUSETTS
✳ Stanley Park of Westfield
400 Western Avenue, Westfield

MICHIGAN
✳ Michigan State University
Horticultural Gardens, E. Lansing

Frances Park Rose Garden
3200 Moores River Dr., Lansing

MINNESOTA
Lake Harriett Rose Garden
Roseway Road & Lake Harriett Blvd.
Minneapolis

MISSISSIPPI
Hattiesburg Area Rose Garden
Univ. of Southern Miss., Hattiesburg

MISSOURI
Capaha Park Rose Garden
Parkdale & Perry Ave., Cape Girardeau

Laura Conyers Smith Rose Garden
5200 Pennsylvania, Kansas City

Missouri Botanical Rose Garden
2345 Tower Grove Ave., St. Louis

MONTANA
Missoula Memorial Rose Garden
Sunset Park, Missoula

NEBRASKA
Lincoln Municipal Rose Garden
Antelope Park, Lincoln

Memorial Park Rose Garden
57th & Underwood Ave., Omaha

NEVADA
Reno Municipal Rose Garden
Idlewild Park, Reno

NEW JERSEY
Brookdale Park Rose Garden
Bloomfield

Colonial Park Rose Garden
Mettlers Road, East Millstone

Lambertus C. Bobbink Memorial
Rose Garden
Thompson Park, Lincroft

NEW MEXICO
Prospect Park Rose Garden
8205 Apache Ave., N. E., Albuquerque

NEW YORK
Edwin De T. Bechtel Memorial
Rose Garden
New York Botanical Garden, Bronx

Cranford Memorial Rose Garden
Brooklyn Botanic Garden, Brooklyn

Sonnenberg Gardens Rose Garden
151 Charlotte Street, Canandaigua

Queens Botanical Garden
43-50 Main Street, Flushing

United Nations Rose Garden
United Nations, New York

Maplewood Park Rose Garden
100 Maplewood Avenue, Rochester

Central Park Rose Garden
Central Park, Schenectady

NORTH CAROLINA
Raleigh Municipal Rose Garden
301 Pogue Street, Raleigh

Reynolda Rose Garden of
Wake Forest University
100 Reynolda Village
Winston-Salem

OHIO
Columbus Park of Roses
3923 N. High Street, Columbus

Kingwood Center
900 Park Ave. West, Mansfield

OKLAHOMA
J. E. Conrad Rose Garden
Honor Heights Park, Muskogee

Municipal Rose Garden
Will Rogers Park
3500 N. W. 36th St., Oklahoma City

✳ Tulsa Municipal Rose Garden
Woodward Park
1370 E. 24th Place, Tulsa

OREGON
Shore Acres State Park
Route 2, Coos Bay

Avery Park Rose Garden
South 15th St., Corvallis

George E. Owen Rose Garden
3 N. Jefferson St., Eugene

✳ International Rose Test Garden
400 S. W. Kingston Ave., Portland

PENNSYLVANIA
Malcolm W. Gross Rose Garden
2700 Parkway Blvd., Allentown

Hershey Rose Gardens
621 Park Avenue, Hershey

Longwood Gardens, Kennett Square

Marion W. Rivinus Rose Garden
Morris Arboretum
9414 Meadowbrook Ave., Philadelphia

✳ Penn State Univ. Rose Garden
301 Tyson, University Park

SOUTH CAROLINA
✳ Edisto Gardens Rose Garden
U. S. 301 South, Orangeburg

TENNESSEE
Warner Park Rose Garden
McCallie Ave., Chattanooga

Memphis Municipal Rose Garden
Audubon Park
750 Cherry Road, Memphis

TEXAS
Samuell-Grand Rose Garden
6200 East Grand Blvd., Dallas

Municipal Rose Garden
1701 Copia Street, El Paso

Fort Worth Botanic Garden
3220 Botanic Garden Dr., Fort Worth

Houston Municipal Rose Garden
1500 Hermann Drive, Houston

Civic League Park Rose Garden
W. Beauregard & Park St., San Angelo

✳ Tyler Municipal Rose Garden
West Front Street, Tyler

UTAH
Territorial Statehouse Rose Garden
50 W. Capitol Ave., Fillmore

Nephi Memorial Rose Garden
100 North 100 East, Nephi

Salt Lake City Municipal Rose Garden
Sugar House Park
1602 E. 21st South, Salt Lake City

VIRGINIA
Arlington Rose Foundation
Bon Air Park
Wilson Blvd. & Lexington St., Arlington

Norfolk Botanical Rose Gardens
Airport Road, Norfolk

Mountain View (Fishburn) Garden
714 13th St., S. W., Roanoke

WASHINGTON
Fairhaven Park Rose Garden
108 Chuckanut Drive, Bellingham

Chehalis Municipal Rose Garden
80 N. E. Cascade, Chehalis

✳ Woodland Park Rose Garden
700 N. 50th Street, Seattle

Manito Park, Rose Hill
West 4, 21st Avenue, Spokane

Point Defiance Park Rose Garden
5402 North Shirley, Tacoma

WEST VIRGINIA
Ritter Park Rose Garden
McCoy Road, Huntington

WISCONSIN
✳ Boerner Botanical Gardens
Whithall Park
5879 South 92nd St.
Hales Corners

CANADA
The Butchart Gardens, Ltd.
Victoria

Hamiton Botanic Gardens
Ontario

✳ All-America Rose Selections Test and
Demonstration Gardens

Index

Bold face indicates most important reference.

Acknowledgments:

American Rose Center, Shreveport, LA; Richard Blissard, President, Portland Rose Society, Portland, OR; Berkeley Municipal Rose Garden, Berkeley, CA; Mrs. Robin Brians, President, Tyler Garden Club, Tyler, TX; Cranbrook Educational Community, Bloomfield Hills, NY; Christine Cress, Troy, MI; Harvey Davidson, Rosarian, Orinda, CA; Beverly Dobson, Secretary Treasurer, Rose Hybridizers Association, Irvington, NY; Filoli Center, Woodside, CA; Sam Goldwater, Lone Star Nursery, Inc., Tyler, TX; A.M. Griner, Tigard, OR; George Haight, Stocking Rose Nursery, San Jose, CA; Don Herzog, Mini Plant Kingdom, Sebastopol, CA; Hodges Gardens, Many, LA; Darrel Johnson, Curator, Portland International Rose Test Garden, Portland, OR; James Kirk, Rosarian, Rose Hills Memorial Park, Whittier, CA; Joseph Klima, Consulting Rosarian, Kentwood, CA; Stanley & Marion Kroll, San Diego, CA; Bob Lawrence, Portland, OR; Ellen Leloy, Consulting Rosarian, Lafayette, CA; Robert Linck, La Jolla, CA; Darley Lisherness, Consulting Rosarian, Piedmont, CA; Dr. Eldon W. Lyle, Plant Pathologist, Texas Rose Research Foundation, Inc., Tyler, TX; James Maxwell, Tigard, OR; Harold Miller, Portland, OR; Jim Miller, Consulting Rosarian, Shreveport, LA; Morcum Amphitheater of Roses, Oakland, CA; Virgil & Wilma Owings, Portland, OR; Planting Fields Arboretum, Oyster Bay, Long Island, NY; Walter Regan Jr., Portland, OR; Paul Reynolds, Portland, OR; George Rose, Director of Public Relations, All-America Rose Selections, Shenandoah, IA; George Shiraki, Consulting Rosarian, San Leandro, CA; Patricia Wiley Stemler, Roses of Yesterday and Today, Watsonville, CA; Carl A. Totemeier, Jr., Horticultural Director, Old Westbury Gardens, Long Island, NY; Mrs. C.J. Traverse, Napa, CA; Tyler Rose Center, Tyler, TX; Charles B. Walker, Portland, OR; Barbara Worl, Bells Books, Palo Alto, CA

We also wish to thank the entire community of rose lovers who so generously contributed their time and experience to this book.